Wit's End

*I Is an Other: The Secret Life of Metaphor
and How It Shapes the Way We See the World*

Geary's Guide to the World's Great Aphorists

*The World in a Phrase:
A Brief History of the Aphorism*

*The Body Electric:
An Anatomy of the New Bionic Senses*

JAMES GEARY

Wit's End

WHAT WIT IS, *HOW* IT WORKS, AND *WHY* WE NEED IT

W. W. NORTON & COMPANY
Independent Publishers Since 1923
New York | London

Excerpt from *Dan Burley's Jive* by Dan Burley, reprinted with permission from Northern Illinois University Press. © 2009 Northern Illinois University Press. Excerpt from *Holding On: Dreamers, Visionaries, Eccentrics, and Other American Heroes* by David Isay and Harvey Wang. Copyright © 1996 by David Isay. Photos copyright © 1996 by Harvey Wang. Foreword copyright © 1996 by Henry Roth. Used by permission of W. W. Norton & Company, Inc. Excerpt from "The Signifying Monkey," from *From My People: 400 Years of African American Folklore*, edited by Daryl Cumber Dance. Copyright © 2002 by Daryl Cumber Dance. Used by permission of W. W. Norton & Company, Inc.

For information about permission to reproduce selections from this book, write to Permissions, W. W. Norton & Company, Inc., 500 Fifth Avenue, New York, NY 10110

For information about special discounts for bulk purchases, please contact W. W. Norton Special Sales at specialsales@wwnorton.com or 800-233-4830

Manufacturing by LSC Communications Harrisonburg
Book design by JAM Design

ISBN 978-0-393-25494-5

W. W. Norton & Company, Inc., 500 Fifth Avenue, New York, N.Y. 10110
www.wwnorton.com

W. W. Norton & Company Ltd., 15 Carlisle Street, London W1D 3BS

2 3 4 5 6 7 8 9 0

The highest wit is wisdom at play.

BRITISH QUARTERLY REVIEW, 1872

CONTENTS

Wit's End

True wit is nature to advantage dress'd,

What oft was thought, but ne'er so well express'd;

Something, whose truth convinc'd at sight we find,

That gives us back the image of our mind.

ALEXANDER POPE

OFT WAS THOUGHT

AN ESSAY IN SIXTY-FOUR LINES

Being the structure and argument of this book,

penned in the heroic couplets

of Alexander Pope

In seeking Wit, lost image of the mind,
Hoping there something of our Selves to find,
For what better guide could an author hope
Than the Wit of Twickenham, Alex Pope?

Pope's darts and barbs are still invaluable,
His definitions still infallible:
Wit thinks at once in poetry and prose
What few say well but everybody knows.

Yet how in putting Wit under the knife
Not talk it to death but bring it to life?
Sad is any anatomy of Wit
When the subject itself expires of it.

Of the solution let there be no doubt:
Strive to make this book what it is about;
Each theme matched to the style in which it's writ,
Thus to show, not tell, the story of Wit.

So each chapter starts with indication
From whither I drew my inspiration,
While detailed sources are kept careful track
In the extensive footnotes at the back.

We begin, before all is said and done,
With true Wit's lowly highest form, the pun,
Which showing word and world as intertwined
Is fertile guano of the wingèd mind.

The science of word play is then explored,
Wherein wits wield their tongues like sharpened swords.
To devise *bon mots* readers are inspired,
Although some assembly may be required.

We celebrate the power of the brain
To insult, enlighten, and entertain,
Through the rhetoric of jive, jazz, and rap
To beguile, to persuade, and cut the crap.

We next conduct the mind to "turning words,"
Sayings that from fixed courses cause a swerve,
Which leads through spins, twists, and misdirection
To unfathomed depths of introspection.

Of worldly wiles there is no full picture
Without Wit's hero-villain: the Trickster,
Who, using guile, cunning, and perfidy,
Slyly triumphs over adversity.

Habit, cruel enemy of invention,
Now lays claim to our complete attention;
That blindness produced when we see by rote,
For which only Wit holds the antidote.

For progress, in the arts or sciences,
Requires seeing through narrow biases,
And creativity so oft depends
On the ingenious use of odds and ends.

Then on, round the world and through the ages,
To the Wit of jesters, fools, and sages;
Those who, in deeds cool and words laconic,
In the tragic discover the comic.

Be like the clown wry, like the serpent wise;
She who is most amused is most alive.
Of all fortune stripped, of all hope bereft,
He tends to end best who begins in jest.

And so, by playful peregrination,
We come, at last, to our destination:
The point at which heart and mind were parted,
The garden path where it all got started.

Wit bids us not see false but face to face,
To fold this ruptured world in one embrace,
To cry if we must, to laugh when we can,
If just to find the way from God to man.

In the beginning was the pun.

SAMUEL BECKETT

ONE BAD APPLE

OR, AN APOLOGY FOR PARONOMASIA

In which the author argues that puns are not
wit's lowest form but its highest expression

ONCE UPON A time, in 382 CE, to be exact, Eve bit into an apple.

Seeing it was good, she offered the apple to Adam, and he also took a bite. Whereupon Adam and Eve's eyes were opened, and they realized they were naked. Ashamed at having broken God's sole commandment not to eat of the Tree of the Knowledge of Good and Evil, Adam and Eve hid themselves when He came walking in the garden.

And the rest, of course, is history.

God in His wrath decreed that henceforth man must earn his daily bread by working the earth and woman must suffer agony in childbirth. As a final punishment, He cast Eve and Adam forever out of Eden.

Prior to the fourth century, however, no one knew exactly which forbidden fruit Eve and Adam ate. Genesis records only that the Tree of the Knowledge of Good and Evil was off-limits; it does not specify what edible flower that tree produced.

Apples appeared in 382 because that's when Pope Damasus I asked Saint Jerome to translate the Old Latin Bible into the simpler Latin Vulgate, which became the definitive edition of the text for the next thousand years. In the Vulgate, the adjectival form of "evil," *malus*, is *malum*, which also happens to be the word for "apple." The similarity between *malum* (evil) and *malum* (apple) prompted Saint Jerome to pick that word to describe what Eve and Adam ate, thereby ushering sin into the world.

The truth is, though, the apple is innocent, and this unjustly maligned fruit's association with original sin comes down to nothing more than a pun.

Puns straddle that happy fault where sound and sense collide, where surface similarities of spelling or pronunciation meet above conflicting seams of meaning. By grafting the idea of evil onto the word for apple, Saint Jerome ensured that every time we recall Adam and Eve's fateful disobedience in the garden we are reminded of the fruit of a deciduous tree of the rose family.

From the beginning, punning has been considered the lowest form of wit, a painful fall from conversational grace. What other form of speech is so widely reviled that we must immediately apologize for using it? "Sorry, no pun intended."

But puns do not deserve such a bitter appellation. Despite its bad reputation, punning is, in fact, among the highest displays of wit. Indeed, puns point to the essence of all true wit—the ability to hold in the mind two different ideas about the same thing at the same time. And the pun's primacy is demonstrated by its strategic use in the oldest sacred stories, texts, and myths.

The Bible is replete with puns, even without Saint Jerome's help. God fashioned Adam from *adamah*, Biblical Hebrew for "earth." Eve's ancient Hebrew name is Havvah, derived from *ahavvah*, which means "longing" or "love" but is also related to the words for "craving," "mischief," and "calamity." Punning was even present at the foundation of the Christian faith itself, when

Jesus famously said he intended to build his church upon Peter, whose name in Aramaic and in Greek means "rock."

In Egyptian mythology, the human race sprang from the sun god Ra's tears; though written differently, the words for "people" and "tears" had the same pronunciation (*remtj*) in ancient Egyptian. The opening verses of the Indian epic the *Ramayana* condemn a hunter who fells a beautiful crane with an arrow, but the same words can also be construed as praising the Hindu god Vishnu for felling the demon Ravana. And the classic Chinese philosophical text *Tao Te Ching* begins with a triple pun: "The way (*tao*) that can be talked about (*tao*) is not the constant Way (*Tao*)."

Punning folds a double knowledge into words. To make and understand a pun, you must grasp two things at once: the primary, apparently intended import of a word or phrase, and the secondary, usually subversive one.

The frisson in the ship captain's reply to the first-class passenger who asks if he can decide for himself whether to help row the lifeboat—"Of course, sir, either oar"—lies in the friction between explicit instruction and implicit threat. The brilliance of the tagline of the Upstate New York town known for its ravines and waterfalls—"Ithaca is gorges"—lies in the simultaneous statement of geological fact and natural beauty.

The best puns have more to do with philosophy than with being funny. Playing with words is playing with ideas, and a likeness between two different terms suggests a likeness between their referents, too. Puns are therefore not mere linguistic coincidences but evidence and expression of a hidden connection—between mind and material, ideas and things, knowing and nomenclature.

Puns are pins on the map tracing the path from word to world.

．　　．　　．　　．

NOT ALL PUNS need to reveal a concealed metaphysical truth. Some are simple homophonic homages, which must be said aloud to be fully appreciated, such as, "When you've seen one shopping center, you've seen 'em all."

Some puns offhandedly master the art of allusion, as in the description of contentment as "the smother of invention."

Some offer deviant definitions; e.g., "earthquake ('ərth,kwāk), n. a topographical error."

And some span more than one language, to wit: the characterization of an elegant frankfurter as a "*haute* dog," a form of wordplay known as macaronic (from the Latin *macaronicus*, meaning "jumble" or "medley"), of which puns about German sausage are generally considered the worst.

Yet even cheesy puns like these show how language is equivocal, two-faced, duplicitous. Many of the simplest and most common words sound the same but have equal and often opposite meanings.

"Fast" means "to move quickly" (She can run *fast*) as well as "to be immobile" (She was stuck *fast*). Both meanings of "cleave" cohere: "to split" (The paddle *cleaves* the water with every stroke) and "to cling" (We *cleave* to hope even when all hope is gone). "Off" conveys both activity and idleness: When the alarm went *off*, I realized I had forgotten to turn it *off*.

What Alexander Pope said of puns—they speak "twice as much by being split"—is true of language as a whole, too.

In this respect, puns pun on human life, which is itself equivocal, two-faced, duplicitous. Everything does double duty. Doors offer exits and entrances; tears come from comedy and tragedy.

James Joyce had a painting of his father's hometown—Cork, Ireland—framed in cork and hung in his Paris apartment, a physical reminder of his notion of the world as a place "where unexpected simultaneities are the rule . . . Words move into words, people into people, incidents into incidents like the ambiguities of a pun, or a dream," according to Richard Ellmann's biography of the author of *Finnegans Wake*, a 600+-page novel made up almost entirely of macaronic puns.

Nor could Shakespeare himself resist a little quibble, as puns were known in his day. There are some 200 puns in *Love's Labour's Lost*, 175 in *Romeo and Juliet*, 150 in each of the Henry IV plays, and upward of 100 in *Much Ado About Nothing* and *All's Well That Ends Well*. The average number of puns in a Shakespeare play is 78.

It was all a bit much for Samuel Johnson, who wrote of the Bard's relish for this form of wordplay, "A quibble is the golden apple for which he will always turn aside from his career, or stoop from his elevation."

But what Johnson could not stomach about puns is the essence of their appeal as wit.

In Act I, Scene IV of *King Lear*, the Fool taunts Lear for being, well, a fool for dividing his kingdom between his two deceitful daughters while disowning his upright third daughter. He asks Lear for an egg, for which he offers to pay the sum of two crowns.

"What two crowns shall they be?" Lear asks.

Then the puns come trippingly from the Fool's tongue.

Having cut the egg and eaten the whites, the Fool answers, he would offer Lear both halves of the yellow yolk, an image of the sundered royal headgear. He then berates Lear for dividing his crown—his kingdom—and giving half to each of his conniving daughters. Finally, he says Lear was stupid to do what he did: "Thou hadst little wit in thy bald crown, / when thou gavest thy golden one away."

In this short speech, the Fool spins four puns from a single word. First, he pivots from "crown," the coin, to "crown," the monarch's mantle. Then he plays off the resemblance between a semicircle of cloven yolk and the broken arc of a golden crown, a visual pun. Then he moves from "crown," a physical object, to "crown," a metaphor for the realm over which a king rules. And he tops it all off by calling Lear a bonehead and numbskull, skipping from "crown" as sovereign domain to "crown" as empty patriarchal pate.

The Fool is not altogether fool, and the pun is not merely a prankish word game.

In stooping to employ the lowly quibble, Shakespeare elevates buried or forgotten senses of words, showing how the names for things intertwine with the things themselves. When he turns aside from balder statement to pursue that golden apple, he makes surprising correlations and uncanny couplings that keep the reader toggling back and forth between meanings. The puns are both launchpads and landing strips for the Fool's daring leaps of thought.

In poems, words rhyme; in puns, ideas rhyme. This is the ultimate test of wittiness: keeping your balance even when you're of two minds.

．　　　．　　　．　　　．

DURING A STINT on the circuit court in Bloomington, Illinois, Abraham Lincoln had occasion to serve with prosecuting attorney Ward Lamon, a man of imposing physical strength who enjoyed challenging colleagues to friendly bouts of wrestling between sessions. One day, while Lamon was wrestling an opponent near the courthouse, his exertions caused a profound rent in the seat of his pants. Being called at just that moment into court, Lamon was unable to redress the situation or effect repairs, so when he rose to address the jury his sartorial misfortune was readily apparent.

The other members of the bar, who had full prospect of Lamon's predicament from their chairs at a long table immediately to the rear of the prosecuting attorney, drew up a subscription to raise funds for a new pair of trousers. They passed the paper down the line from lawyer to lawyer, each one signing his name and pledging some absurd amount to cover Lamon's embarrassment.

When the paper came before Lincoln, he quietly examined it, picked up his pen, wrote his name and under it a note of regret about his inability to render any pecuniary aid: "I can contribute nothing to the end in view."

Lincoln loved puns. Strolling down Pennsylvania Avenue with the president, Secretary of State William H. Seward happened to note a sign bearing the name of one "T. R. Strong." "Ha!" Lincoln cried, "T. R. Strong but coffee are stronger."

Upon receiving a letter from a Catholic priest asking him to suspend the sentence of a man due to hang the next day, Lincoln observed, "If I don't suspend it tonight, the man will surely be suspended tomorrow."

Lincoln's wordplay offers admirable instruction in how wit actually works.

Sigmund Freud shared Lincoln's fascination for punning, and in *Jokes and Their Relationship to the Unconscious* he offers a pun from Heinrich Heine's "The Baths of Lucca" as a model for the mechanics of wit. In the story, the humble Hamburg lottery agent Hirsch-Hyacinth meets the famous Baron Rothschild and later boasts of how well the fabulously wealthy banker treated him, "just as if I were his equal, quite famillionaire."

The coining of the term "famillionaire" is a vivid example of "the peculiar process of condensation and fusion" Freud believed characterized puns in particular and wit in general. In condensing "famillionaire" from "familiar" and "millionaire," Heine fused two definitions into a new double meaning, a meaning all the more striking for having been distilled from such disparate sources. The combination makes two things seen together seem quite strange that are, when regarded apart, seen as quite commonplace.

All puns, including Lincoln's, operate in this way. By bringing together two distinct senses of "suspend"—one legal and metaphorical, the other physical and literal—in the same mental space, Lincoln blended realms of understanding and interpretation that in conventional thinking remain separate. Through deft juxtapositions like this, puns reveal previously unseen relations among things. This reordering of ordinary associations, this upsetting of the applecart of expectations, affords the mind sudden alternative points of view on subjects and situations it thought it knew.

The relationship between wit and knowledge is embedded in the word's etymology. Derived from the Sanskrit verb *vid*, "to perceive," "wit" occurs in Latin as *vidēre* and in Greek as *idein*, both of which mean "to see"; hence, the word "witness." *Vid* is also the source for the German word for wit, *Witz*. (The German title of Freud's book on the subject is *Der Witz und seine Beziehung zum Unbewußten* or, literally, "Wit and Its Relationship to the Unconscious.") And *vid* is the root of *witan*, Old English for "to know or understand," whence comes the word "wisdom."

Words like "outwit" and "quick-witted" hint at the link between wit and knowing, while words like "dimwit," "nitwit," "witless," and "unwitting" hint at the link between wit and not knowing. We have our wits about us if we are street-smart, savvy, or shrewd. We live by our wits when we devise impromptu solutions to sticky situations or evade seemingly inevitable consequences. We can be scared out of our wits and, sadly, we can also reach our wit's end.

The power of wit to provide insight and information is precisely what Isaac Tuxton, a scholar otherwise lost to history, celebrated in the pages of the *Irish Monthly* in 1877. "Delighted surprise is the common immediate sensation following fresh knowledge of an elevated or curious kind," he wrote. "Whenever resemblances or relations are established between ideas, knowledge of some kind is communicated. Wit establishes such relations. Knowledge shows us what things are, how they are or might be, how things may be done and ends gained. Wit does the same. Therefore wit is knowledge, and communicates knowledge."

Etymologically—and psychologically—wit and wisdom are the same thing.

.   .   .   .

CHARLES LAMB ONCE remarked that, when the time came for him to leave this earth, his fondest wish would be to draw his last breath through a pipe and exhale it in a pun. And he was a prodigious punster. Once, when a friend, about to introduce the notoriously shy English essayist to a group of strangers, asked him, "Promise, Lamb, not to be so sheepish," he replied, "I wool."

Lamb and his close friend Samuel Taylor Coleridge shared a passion for punning, not just as a fireside diversion but as a model for the witty workings of the imaginative mind. "All men who possess at once active fancy, imagination, and a philosophical spirit, are prone to punning," Coleridge declared. He planned a spirited defense of the widely impugned practice, to be called "An Apology for Paronomasia," the Greek word for "pun," drawn from *para* ("beside") and *onomasia* ("to name").

Coleridge considered punning an essentially poetic act, exhibiting sensitivity to the subtlest, most distant relationships as well as an acrobatic exercise of intelligence, connecting things formerly believed to be unconnected. "A ridiculous likeness leads to the detection of a true analogy" is the way he explained it.

The novelist and cultural critic Arthur Koestler picked up Coleridge's idea and used it as the basis for his theory of creativity.

Koestler regarded the pun, which he described as "two strings of thought tied together by an acoustic knot," as among the most powerful proofs of "bisociation," the process of discovering similarity in the dissimilar that he suspected was the foundation for all creativity. A pun, or indeed any instance of wit, "compels us to perceive the situation in two self-consistent but incompatible frames of reference at the same time," Koestler argued. "While this unusual condition lasts, the event is not, as is normally the case, associated with a single frame of reference, but *bisociated* with two."

For Koestler, the ability to simultaneously view a situation through multiple frames of reference is the source of all creative breakthroughs—in the sciences, the arts, and the humanities.

Isaac Newton was bisociating when, as he sat in contemplative mood in his garden, he watched an apple fall to the ground and understood it as both the unremarkable fate of a piece of ripe fruit and a startling demonstration of the law of gravity. Paul Cézanne was bisociating when he depicted his astonishing apples both as naturalistic, meticulously arranged produce and as numinous, otherworldly objects that existed only in his pigments and brushstrokes. Saint Jerome was bisociating when he alighted on *malum* as the perfect word to describe the actual fruit Adam and Eve ate as well as their bad taste in partaking of the Tree of the Knowledge of Good and Evil in the first place.

There is no sharp boundary splitting the wit of the scientist, inventor, or improviser from that of the artist, the sage, or the jester. The creative experience moves seamlessly from the "Aha!" of scientific discovery to the "Ah" of aesthetic insight to the "Ha-ha" of the pun and the punch line. "Comic discovery is paradox stated—scientific discovery is paradox resolved," Koestler wrote.

Bisociation is central to creative thought, Koestler believed, because "the conscious and unconscious processes underlying creativity are essentially combinatorial activities—the bringing together of previously separate areas of knowledge and experience."

This is precisely how wit was understood in the sixteenth and seventeenth centuries when the word was used to describe innovative thinking—something more akin to intellect or consciousness than to glibness or flippancy, a state of mind rather than just a sense of humor.

Lately, though, wit's been whittled down to a sliver of what it really is. "Witty" has come to mean merely funny, and a "wit" is just someone with a knack for snappy comebacks.

True wit is richer, cannier, more riddling.

Wit can be visual as well as verbal, physical as well as intellectual. There is the kinetic wit of physical comedians, the serendipitous wit of scientists, the crafty wit of inventors, the optical wit of artists, and the metaphysical wit of philosophers. Wit is the faculty of mind that integrates knowledge and experience, fuses divided worlds, and links the like with the unlike. The pun is at once the most profound and the most pedestrian example of wit at work.

Coleridge never did complete his planned apology, but Lamb

did write several essays on punning before he breathed his last, including one entitled "That the Worst Puns Are the Best," in which he vigorously defended paronomasia, arguing that "the pun is not bound by the laws which limit nicer wit. It is a pistol let off at the ear; not a feather to tickle the intellect."

Let the pun be the starting gun for this renaissance of true wit.

THIRTY-FIVE DAYS IN MAY

*Being a consideration of verbal wit, its similarity to fencing,
and the collaboration between speaker and listener
necessary for the mutual enjoyment of witticisms,
written in the manner of a dramatic dialogue*

CHARACTERS

DENIS DIDEROT: *eighteenth century French philosopher, essayist, and playwright.*

ANNE LOUISE GERMAINE DE STAËL-HOLSTEIN: *late
eighteenth and early nineteenth century French-Swiss
author, literary theorist, and political thinker.*

SCENE

*Madame de Staël and Denis Diderot are walking together
after attending a dinner party at the home of De
Staël's father, banker and statesman Jacques Necker, at
which Diderot had been insulted by another guest.
Diderot was so flustered by the affront that he only
thought of a clever retort as he was walking down the
stairs on his way out. The encounter led him to devise
the term "l'esprit d'escalier," "the wit of the stair-
case," for the experience of thinking of a witty come-
back only after it is too late to deliver it.*

DIDEROT: The man of sensibility, like me, completely overcome by the argument against him, loses his head and only recovers when he gets to the bottom of the stairs.

DE STAËL: That's the difference between plays and real life—thinking time.

DIDEROT: Yes, I need to be able to think faster on my feet.

DE STAËL: And on your posterior, lest churlish dinner guests make an ass of you.

DIDEROT: Quite. But for my part, I confess, wit loses its respect with me, when I see it in company with malice.

DE STAËL: Pshaw! There's no possibility of being witty without a little ill-nature: The malice of a good thing is the barb that makes it stick. What's required at such a moment is known in fencing as a *riposte*—a quick, robust return thrust. Fencing is, in fact, an apt metaphor for verbal wit.

DIDEROT: Really? How so?

DE STAËL: In English, many of the words for wit come from French fencing terms. Someone with a sharp tongue has a *rapier* wit. A wit's unfunny sidekick is his *foil*. A witty verbal attack is a *sally*, which we *parry* with a *riposte* of our own.

DIDEROT: Yes, and in French we call the knob at the tip of a sword the *fleuret*, or blossom, another word for a witty remark, or *bon mot*.

DE STAËL: Indeed. Even *touch*, a hit with the blade, is drawn from the vocabulary of fencing—from *touché*, which we say in acknowledgment of a superior argument or an especially cutting remark. The riposte is wit as weapon.

DIDEROT: Ah, yes, I see your point.

DE STAËL: In *On Fencing*, Italian master Aldo Nadi described the sport as "a sparkling exchange of wits, with action and counteraction taking place at an almost unbelievable speed . . . It is excitement, exhilaration, pure joy of the spirit."

DIDEROT: I found this evening's exchange more humiliating than exhilarating, and nothing sparkled about my wit until the contest was long finished.

DE STAËL: Perhaps you could learn a thing or two from fencing. Nadi believed fencing was as much a psychological as a physical exercise, that the fencer's blade is an extension of the fencer's mind. "To win," he wrote, "the fencer must first outwit his adversary."

DIDEROT: Now, that is something I would dearly like to learn. Lay on, De Staël.

DE STAËL: Very well. Fencing is a mix of etiquette and brute force. The bell guard, the section of the sword between the blade and the handle, hides a little grip. Grasp this firmly, as if pointing a pistol, but with finesse, as if holding a pen. Handle words the same way—lightly but with exquisite precision.

DIDEROT: That is easier said than done.

DE STAËL: Footwork calibrates the space between you and your opponent, manipulating your respective positions to bring him within striking distance. Your touch must be felt before it is seen.

DIDEROT: "Float like a butterfly, sting like a bee; the hands can't hit what the eyes can't see."

DE STAËL: Then, when you attack, lunge suddenly, with a snake's casual grace, your pointed words aimed directly at your opponent's chest. Conception and execution must be simultaneous, and a pungent remark must hit the target before the speaker seems to have had time to think.

DIDEROT: Make his breast a sheath for thy steel, Germaine.

DE STAËL: And remember, hits are only scored with the tip of the blade. Hits with the flat of the blade are ignored. The same is true of wit. Witticisms are surgical strikes; cruder, broader strokes do not count.

DIDEROT: That's all well and good, but how does it work in practice?

DE STAËL: First, detach yourself from any emotion that might induce you to lash out. The timely, well-aimed thrust ends a contest more surely than any angry slashing about. If you flail, you fail.

DIDEROT: Yes, I must be on guard for that.

DE STAËL: Nadi counseled a kind of studied nonchalance, retaining your composure in response to an attack yet remaining ready "to strike suddenly, passing instantly from apparently total casualness and relaxation to irresistible speed and power, controlling the point perfectly as you do so."

DIDEROT: That sounds very much like what Nadi's countryman Baldassare Castiglione called *sprezzatura*, a certain nonchalance, so as to conceal all art and make whatever one does or says appear to be without effort and almost without any thought about it.

DE STAËL: That's it exactly. Castiglione's *The Book of the Courtier* is more than just a Renaissance manual of aristocratic manners; it's a primer on verbal wit. And some of his tips might come in handy the next time you find yourself sparring at a dinner party. Among witticisms, Castiglione wrote, "Those are very elegant which depend on turning someone's own sarcastic remarks against him."

DIDEROT: Turn a put-down into a comeuppance?

DE STAËL: Precisely. Once, a Plains Indian had just placed an offering of food on a fresh grave when a white man approached and asked, "Do you really expect the dead man to come up and eat that food?" "Yes," the Indian replied, "as soon as your dead come up to smell the flowers you place on their graves."

DIDEROT: That smarts.

DE STAËL: Another tactic "consists in a certain dissimulation, when we say one thing and tacitly we imply another." English film director Anthony Asquith introduced Jean Harlow, the platinum blond 1930s Hollywood star, to his mother, Lady Margot Asquith, author and wife of longtime British prime minister Herbert Asquith. Harlow mispronounced Lady Margot's first name, sounding the final "t," as in "forgot." "The 't' is silent, my dear," Asquith snipped, "as in Harlow."

DIDEROT: Dissimulation is the sincerest form of effrontery.

DE STAËL: Another method is "very short, and consists solely of quick and sharp sayings . . . or in biting ones; and unless they sting a little, they are not felicitous." In the 1950s, British philosopher J. L. Austin presented a paper on linguistics at Columbia University in which he pointed out that, while many languages have double negatives that make a positive (e.g., I do not disagree with Welsh crooner Tom Jones's observation, "It's not unusual to be loved by anyone"), no example existed of a language in which two positives make a negative. From the back of the auditorium Columbia philosophy professor Sidney Morgenbesser, known for his mordant wit, stage-whispered, "Yeah, yeah."

DIDEROT: Ha! That Morgenbesser could really do things with words.

DE STAËL: Another move "occurs when we expect to hear one thing and the one who is talking says something different, and this is called the 'unexpected retort.'" Recall the first televised debate of the 1984 U.S. presidential campaign, when Democratic Party candidate Walter Mondale suggested incumbent Republican Ronald Reagan was too old to serve. Reagan was then seventy-three, the oldest president in American history; Mondale was fifty-six and had served as Jimmy Carter's vice president. Reagan wasn't ready with a riposte at that first encounter.

DIDEROT: It was *l'esprit d'escalier* all over again.

DE STAËL: Two weeks later, though, in the second debate, Henry Trewhitt of the *Baltimore Sun* again raised the issue of age, asking the president if he was still up to the job. "I will not make age an issue of this campaign," he replied. "I am not going to exploit, for political purposes, my opponent's youth and inexperience." Mondale lost the election in a landslide.

DIDEROT: Castigation à la Castiglione.

DE STAËL: In fencing terminology, these stratagems might be described as parry, feint, lunge, and riposte—all delivered with the sparkle of *sprezzatura*.

DIDEROT: Very instructive. But can't anyone be witty with a team of speechwriters and two weeks to prepare?

DE STAËL: Perhaps. But Reagan was also a gifted improviser. As a young radio broadcaster in the 1930s, he used to call the Chicago Cubs play-by-play from telegraph dispatches, without actually seeing the games. Once, when the wire went dead in the middle of an at-bat, he improvised the longest sequence of back-to-back foul balls in Major League history until the connection was restored. To be ready with an off-the-cuff remark, keep always something up your sleeve.

DIDEROT: But how do you learn to ad lib like that?

DE STAËL: Making puns is not a bad place to start.

DIDEROT: Puns? I thought they were the lowest form of wit.

DE STAËL: Which is why they are the foundation for all higher forms. Do you consider Georges de Bièvre a lowly wit?

DIDEROT: Indeed not. I confess to having spent many an agreeable hour with the 1770 edition of his *Almanac of Puns*.

DE STAËL: Do you know what de Bièvre said when, encountering Louis XVI in the gardens at Versailles, the king demanded: "You, who make puns on everybody, make one on me"?

DIDEROT: "Your Majesty is not a subject."

DE STAËL: A brilliant riposte, is it not?

DIDEROT: Indeed it is.

DE STAËL: Fencers spend months perfecting their stances and practicing their lunges before ever touching a sword. Reagan spent the time between the first and second debates sharpening his blade. Badinage favors the prepared mind, and a punning regimen trains the brain for wit.

DIDEROT: Please describe a typical workout.

DE STAËL: You can do this exercise on your own, but it's much more fun in a group. It makes for a nice dinner party diversion, too, not unlike Japanese *renga* composition games, in which guests take turns improvising the alternating three- and two-line stanzas of the poem.

DIDEROT: Yes, there were similar verse competitions in ancient Greece. At parties, one person started a poem with a few lines in a specific form and the rest had to continue the poem in that same form. The winner received a laurel wreath, as I recall, and the losers had brine poured in their wine.

DE STAËL: For us, the bitter taste of defeat will suffice. Here's how it works. Choose a category, any category, then come up with as many puns as you can, as quickly as you can, within that category. If the category is, say, "body parts," you might say, "Eyebrows the Web when doing research" or "If you kneed money, I'll lend you some dough."

DIDEROT: Very clever.

DE STAËL: The game goes on like this until everyone has had a chance to pun. Whoever can't make a pun is out. Then you move on to the next category. Food is another popular category: "Lettuce leave this plaice and never return." Want to try it?

DIDEROT: Do I have a choice?

DE STAËL: Start with an easy category, like animals. Go.

DIDEROT: Um . . . Nothing comes to mind.

DE STAËL: "There was pandamonium at the zoo when the bamboo ran out."

DIDEROT: Um, nothing. I'm so boring.

DE STAËL: Boaring is great! What do you call a horn-less African water mammal notorious for its insincer-ity? A "hippocrite."

DIDEROT: Ugh. Let's see . . . Nope, still nothing. This is unbearable.

DE STAËL: Good. Try another category.

DIDEROT: Huh?

DE STAËL: Plants.

DIDEROT: What?

DE STAËL: "*Oaklahoma!* is my favorite musical."

DIDEROT: Um . . . I fear I'm not cut out for this pun-ning stuff. I'm stumped.

DE STAËL: Excellent! Now that you've got the hang of it, shall we consider how punning quickens the wit?

DIDEROT: Yes, that would be a relief.

DE STAËL: Ooh, you are good.

DIDEROT: What?

DE STAËL: Are you familiar with the remote associates test, or RAT, the measure of creativity developed by psychologist Sarnoff Mednick in the 1960s?

DIDEROT: I confess I am not.

DE STAËL: Well, a RAT involves finding the missing term that links a cluster of three words. Given the words "cake," "blue," and "cottage," for example, the missing term would be . . . ?

DIDEROT: "Cheese," of course.

DE STAËL: "Desert," "ice," "spell"?

DIDEROT: Ah, that's more difficult . . . "Dry"!

DE STAËL: Correct. One more: "Jump," "kill," "bliss"?

DIDEROT: Hmmm . . . "Joy"?

DE STAËL: Right. Mednick theorized that creative

thinking operates via "the forming of associative elements into new combinations which either meet specified requirements or are in some way useful." When you solve a RAT, your brain swiftly shuffles through all its associations with those three words until it alights on a missing term they all share. That's pretty much how punning and verbal wit more generally work as well. When Louis XVI demanded a royal pun of de Bièvre, he sprinted through all the associations around the king he could think of until he hit upon the combination of "subject" (as in "person under discussion") and "subject" (as in "person governed by a monarch").

DIDEROT: So, wit is simply a knack for making novel combinations from more or less familiar associations?

DE STAËL: Yes, but as the name of Mednick's test suggests, the more remote the association, the wittier the remark. Groucho's quip upon entering a restaurant and seeing a previous spouse at another table—"Marx spots the ex"—is so witty because it twists a familiar saying to fit a very unfamiliar setting. Stick with the RAT and watch how increasingly distant associations germinate. What associations do you have with the word "leaf"?

DIDEROT: Let's see . . . "Leaf," "tree," "branch," and "fall" spring to mind.

DE STAËL: What else?

DIDEROT: Well . . . "Leaf," "tree," "maple," "syrup." "Leaf," "book," *"Ulysses,"* "Bloom." How's that?

DE STAËL: Anything even more remote?

DIDEROT: Um . . . "Leaf," "tree," "family," "Uncle Jack." "Leaf," "table," "chair," "electric." I'm running out of juice here. Last one . . . "Leaf," "Erikson," "Vikings," "Norway."

DE STAËL: Excellent. See how, from the same starting point, the sequences branch off in utterly different directions? In less than sixty seconds you went from a plant's blade-like vascular organ to an Icelandic explorer said to have arrived in North America five hundred years before Columbus. Widening your aperture of associations expands the number of possible ripostes.

DIDEROT: In theory, this all makes sense. But isn't verbal wit of the kind you describe limited to a select few—Groucho, Castiglione, and others of that ilk?

DE STAËL: Not at all. Some are faster than others on the draw, yes, but everyone instinctively understands a witty remark even if they might feel ill-equipped to deliver one. That's because to "get" a witticism you must take the same mental path as the person who said it.

DIDEROT: How so?

DE STAËL: Which branch of the army do babies join?

DIDEROT: I beg your pardon?

DE STAËL: The infantry.

DIDEROT: Ah, very droll.

DE STAËL: You got the joke instantly, did you not?

DIDEROT: Unfortunately, yes.

DE STAËL: And how did you get it? By understanding the associations between a specific area of military service and a synonym for a newborn child.

DIDEROT: I guess so, yes.

DE STAËL: Well, whoever invented that remark understood those same things, too. That person followed the path of associations forward, so to speak, and you followed it back. The journey and destination are identical; only the direction is different. A witticism only works if the listener becomes an accomplice of the speaker.

DIDEROT: I see. "To penetrate a thought and to produce a thought are almost the same action," as our friend Joseph Joubert put it.

DE STAËL: Just so. And Joubert also wrote, "A thought is a thing as real as a cannon ball," and that, my friend, accounts for verbal wit's explosive impact, which we can see at play in China, where there are thirty-five days in May.

DIDEROT: Thirty-five days in May?

DE STAËL: Yes. All mention of June fourth, the date in 1989 on which the Tiananmen Square massacre took place, is forbidden. Chinese circumvent the ban by talking about the events of May thirty-fifth, four days after the last day in May, the thirty-first.

DIDEROT: A feint to sidestep censors.

DE STAËL: The Communist Party deploys sophisticated software to identify and delete politically sensitive words and phrases from the Internet. But the Chinese evade the "Ministry of Truth," as government censors are known, through a variation on the RAT.

DIDEROT: Please explain.

DE STAËL: Since the Chinese language consists of characters rather than letters, one popular strata- gem is to use a word that shares a character with a censored word as a proxy for the banned term. In 2013 and 2014, when Zhou Yongkang, a former member of the Politburo Standing Committee, the Communist Party's senior decision-making body, was under investigation for corruption, any post mentioning his name was quickly deleted. So people began referring to him as Kang Shifu, or Master Kang, the name of a popular instant noodle brand that also includes the character *kang*.

DIDEROT: Did it work?

DE STAËL: Until the censors caught on, as censors do. Soon all references to Master Kang were getting zapped, too. So people substituted a word close to the meaning of the newly proscribed word; thus, Master Kang became *fangbiànmiàn*, the generic term for "instant noodles."

DIDEROT: And was that code also broken?

DE STAËL: Of course, and when it was, people swapped the *zhou* in Zhou Yongkang for a homophone, a character with the same pronunciation but a totally different meaning, resulting in the nickname "Rice Porridge" Yongkang, who was eventually convicted of abuse of power and sentenced to life in prison.

DIDEROT: From former Politburo member to bowl of rice porridge—that's quite a trail of associations.

DE STAËL: And no one needed a glossary to follow it.

DIDEROT: So, wit is equally distributed among the population, it's just that some find it better to give than to receive. And punch line trumps party line every time.

DE STAËL: Wit is an instrument one likes to play that revives the spirit, a quick give-and-take of pleasure, a way of speaking as soon as one thinks, of rejoicing in oneself and in the immediate present—in short, the ability to produce at will a kind of lightning, which, emitting a shower of sparks, relieves the excess of liveliness in some and rouses others from their apathy.

DIDEROT: And offers those suffering from *l'esprit d'escalier* a remedy, so they will never be at a loss to say something good and well suited to those with whom they are speaking, something that will move them discreetly to mirth or introspection.

DE STAËL: Indeed, my dear Diderot. But enough of this banter. I'm meeting friends at the Algonquin for a nightcap, where, I'm told, rather excellent jazz and rap musicians will be improvising. Would you like to join me?

DIDEROT: Why, are you coming apart?

DE STAËL: Touché.

Exeunt, laughing.

Think long, think wrong.

WYNTON MARSALIS

WATCHERS AT THE GATES OF MIND

WIT AND ITS RELATION TO WITZELSUCHT,

MALAPROPISMS, AND BIPOLAR DISORDER

Being an overview of how wit might work in

the brain, presented as a scientific paper

ABSTRACT: *Witzelsucht*, a term derived from the German words for "wit" (*Witz*) and "sickness" or "addiction" (*suchen*), is characterized by the compulsion to make bad jokes and terrible puns and occurs in patients with brain damage or neurological disease. Study of this condition may yield insights into the neural mechanisms underlying the associative, improvisational intelligence necessary to generate and appreciate non-pathological expressions of wit, suggesting potential answers to questions that have long puzzled researchers, including, "Why don't cannibals eat clowns?"

KEY WORDS: Friedrich Schiller, *Witzelsucht*, Groucho Marx glasses, plastic dog poop, malapropisms, Archie Bunkerisms, default and executive networks, flight of ideas, over-inclusive thinking, Robin Williams, Joke and Story Completion Test, incongruity, asparagus

In the late eighteenth century, German jurist and patron of the arts Christian Gottfried Körner built a little theater in his Dresden home, where he and his friends—who included Mozart, Goethe, and Friedrich Schiller—staged plays and chamber concerts. Schiller lived in the house for a while, some of his dramas received private premieres there, and he and Körner maintained a lively correspondence throughout their lives.

In 1788, in response to a letter from Körner complaining of creative block, Schiller diagnosed his friend's problem in a way that anticipates contemporary neurobiological insights into how wit—the ability to hold in the mind two different ideas about the same thing at the same time—might work in the brain.

"The reason for your complaint," Schiller wrote, "lies in the constraint which your intelligence imposes upon your imagination . . . It is harmful for the creative work of the mind, if the intelligence inspects too closely the ideas already pouring in, as it were, at the gates. Regarded by itself, an idea may be very trifling and very adventurous, but it perhaps becomes important on account of one that follows it; perhaps in certain connection with others, which seem equally absurd, it is capable of forming a very useful construction. The intelligence cannot judge all these things if it does not hold them steadily long enough to see them in connection with the others. In the case of a creative mind, however, the intelligence has withdrawn its watchers from the gates, the ideas rush in pell-mell, and it is only then that the great heap is looked over and critically examined."[1]

Freud cites this passage in *The Interpretation of Dreams*

1 Cited in: Freud S. The interpretation of dreams. Introduction by A. A. Brill. New York: Macmillan; 1913, pp. 85–86.

to explain the way he believed people suppress troublesome or traumatic thoughts before they become conscious, and the way these thoughts slip past the mind's sentries and into our dreams. He developed the technique of "free association"—sharing thoughts, fantasies, and other forms of ideation without first deliberating over them—to coax suppressed material from the unconscious.

Uncensored access to associations, conscious and unconscious, is essential to wit, and an extreme form of something very much like Schiller's withdrawal of the watchers at the gates seems to occur in the brains of individuals diagnosed with *Witzelsucht*, in which patients compulsively share dreadful puns, facetious jokes, and socially inappropriate wisecracks. Study of the neurobiology of *Witzelsucht* may yield insights into the neurological mechanisms underlying the associative,

improvisational intelligence necessary to generate and appreciate non-pathological expressions of wit.

In neuropsychiatric disease and brain damage, the ability to create and detect puns, jokes, and other witticisms is often impaired. In some cases, however, an abnormal increase in punning and joking is observed, with some patients developing *Witzelsucht*. The condition has been identified as resulting from brain tumors, strokes, infections, and other lesions involving the frontal lobe, particularly the right orbitofrontal region, which previous research has indicated plays an important role in humor appreciation.

Granadillo and Mendez studied two patients with brain disorders and subsequent symptoms of *Witzelsucht*.[2] In Case 1, a sixty-nine-year-

2 Granadillo ED, Mendez MF. Pathological joking or witzelsucht revisited. Journal of Neuropsychiatry and Clinical Neurosciences 2016; 28(3): 162–167.

old man presented with, among other conditions, a sub-arachnoid hemorrhage of undetermined etiology and a lacunar stroke in the left caudate nucleus. After onset, the patient displayed pronounced behavioral changes consistent with *Witzelsucht*. He compulsively punned, made borderline offensive remarks, and became excessively familiar with strangers.

The caudate nucleus is implicated in a variety of cognitive and motor functions, including associative learning (e.g., goldfish and dogs are associated as pets; postal workers and dogs are associated as enemies) and inhibitory control (e.g., the ability to resist clicking on salacious headlines). Case 1's overactive punning and inability to keep his verbal associations to himself offers a possible causal connection between selective brain damage and symptoms of wit gone awry.

Eventually, Case 1's relent-less joking became an issue of contention with his wife. He woke her up nearly every night to share his latest *bon mot* and responded to even the most mundane requests with waggish ripostes. For example, when his wife asked him to shut the bedroom window because it was cold outside, he replied, "And if I shut the window, will it get warmer outside?"[3]

At his wife's insistence, the man began meticulously cataloguing his witticisms in a notebook instead of delivering them in the middle of the night. At interview, he shared the notebook, which was crammed with jokes, puns, and riddles, many of which featured sexual or scatological content (Table 1).

In Case 2, a fifty-seven-year-old man began constantly joking, laughing, and singing

3 Bermant C. What's the joke? A study of Jewish humor through the ages. London: Weidenfeld and Nicolson; 1986, p. 242.

during the last few years of his life. After the patient's death, his wife discovered scores of Groucho Marx glasses, spinning bow ties, hand buzzers, and squirting lapel flowers in their garage. Autopsy showed asymmetric frontotemporal atrophy and Pick's disease, a form of progressive dementia affecting neurons in the frontal and temporal neocortex.

The frontotemporal region, which extends roughly from behind the outer edge of the eyebrow to behind the ear, is implicated in personality and language as well as the regulation of emotions and behavior. Damage to this area can produce a diverse array of corresponding symptoms: wild personality changes, language deficits, socially inappropriate behavior, and emotional withdrawal.

TABLE 1.
Selected Jokes and Puns Presented by Case 1

Why did the woman nickname her lover "Amaretto"?
Because he was a fancy liquor.
What's the last thing that goes through an insect's mind when it hits a windshield?
Its butt.
When the fisherman's daughter saw my rod she reeled.
What do you get when you cut a comedian in two?
A half-wit.
What did the proctologist say to his therapist?
I deal with assholes all day.

Other research teams have studied similar patients. Chen and colleagues reported the case of a Chinese man who developed *Witzelsucht* after a right putaminal hemorrhage that might have severed the fibers connecting the paramedian thalamus and the orbitofrontal cortex.[4] He was outspoken and prankish—he took particular delight in placing plastic dog poop in the hospital corridor—and insisted on addressing his caregivers as famous Chinese historical figures. He referred to his attending physician as K'ung-Ming, a legendary general known for his battlefield cunning, and the rest of the nursing staff as "K'ung-Ming's soldiers."

The putamen is directly connected to the caudate nucleus, which was damaged in Granadillo and Mendez's Case 1, so the symptoms of a damaged putamen overlap with those of a damaged caudate nucleus. The thalamus is a brain hub where nearly all sensory information arrives on its way to perceptual

processing. The function of the orbitofrontal cortex, located behind the eyebrows, remains somewhat difficult to specify, but it is implicated in thinking about the future and planning, among other things.

Though distinct from *Witzelsucht*, malapropisms—the inadvertent substitution, often to comic effect, of words that sound alike but have different meanings—may also be related to neurobiological trauma. The term derives from Richard Sheridan's 1775 play *The Rivals*, in which one of the characters, Mrs. Malaprop, continually misspeaks in this way. "Why, murder's the matter! Slaughter's the matter! Killing's the matter! But he can tell you the perpendiculars," Mrs. Malaprop exclaims at one point in the drama. She also describes another character as "headstrong as an allegory on the banks of the Nile."[5]

4 Chen Y-C, Tseng Y-C, and Pai M-C. Witzelsucht after right putaminal hemorrhage: a case report. Acta Neurologica Taiwanica. 2005; 14(4): 195–200.

5 Sheridan RB. The rivals. Mineola (NY): Dover; 1998, pp. 56, 34.

The condition is perhaps better known today as "Archie Bunker syndrome," after the lead character in the sitcom *All in the Family*, broadcast on American television from 1971 to 1979. In one episode, Archie (Carroll O'Connor) refers to the end of his wife Edith's (Jean Stapleton) menstrual cycle as the "mentalpause." In another, Archie tries to prove he has not had an extramarital affair by averring that sexual relations had not been "constipated."

Mendez reported the case of a fifty-three-year-old man afflicted with Archie Bunker syndrome.[6] When asked about the nature of the clinic at which he was being treated, he described it as "phallic" instead of neurologic. He also characterized his symptoms as the result of a "medieval condition" rather than a medical one. Positron emission tomography (PET) showed marked bifrontal and mild bitemporal hypometabolism consistent with frontotemporal dementia. Thus, the same frontotemporal regions previously discussed as relevant to personality, language, and inhibition were damaged in this patient, too.

Witzelsucht, malapropisms, and Archie Bunker syndrome may provide instructive models for how wit works in brains not compromised by neurological disease or trauma.

Raichle and colleagues posited the existence of a "default network" in the brain that prevails when an individual is awake and alert yet not engaged in tasks that demand focused attention.[7] The default network is thought to be active during states like daydreaming and mind-wandering, when attention is diffuse and the

6 Mendez MF. Malapropisms, or "The Archie Bunker Syndrome," and frontotemporal dementia. Journal of Neuropsychiatry and Clinical Neuroscience. 2011; 23(4): E3.

7 Raichle M et al. A default mode of brain function. Proceedings of the National Academy of Sciences. 2001; 98(2): 676–682.

brain gleans information from a broad array of internal and external sources.[8]

During the performance of tasks that demand focused attention, however, the activity of the default network is attenuated, and the brain's "executive network" asserts control. The executive network is thought to be active in selecting and monitoring goal-directed behaviors, such as reasoning, planning, and problem-solving.

Viewed through Schiller's metaphor for creative work, "imagination" corresponds to the associative, improvisational thinking characteristic of the default network and "intelligence" corresponds to the linear, deliberative thinking characteristic of the executive network (Figure 1).

In patients displaying symptoms of *Witzelsucht*, neurological damage may disable the executive network, permanently withdrawing its watchers from the gates. Freed from the brain's normal system of inhibitory control, the default network may be at liberty to indulge in the kind of unbridled punning, socially inappropriate behavior, and general japery the executive network might otherwise constrain.

A role for the default network has also been suggested in musical and lyrical improvisation, both of which rely on the same type of freewheeling, associative intelligence required to produce puns and jokes.

Limb and Braun used functional magnetic resonance imaging (fMRI) to examine improvisation in professional jazz pianists. The team put pianists in an fMRI scanner and asked them to play memorized passages and to improvise. While improvising, the default networks in

8 Buckner RL et al. The brain's default network anatomy, function, and relevance to disease. Annals of the N.Y. Academy of Science. 2008; 1124: 1–38.

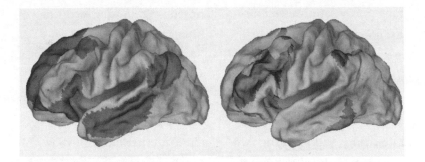

Figure 1. Left: The default network, indicated by darker shaded areas in the upper left and bottom foreground of this brain image. Right: The executive network, concentrated in the darker shaded area in the left-center region of this brain image.

the pianists' brains showed heightened activity while their executive networks showed diminished activity.[9]

Liu and colleagues performed a similar experiment with rappers, who were put in an fMRI scanner and asked to recite prewritten material from memory and to freestyle; i.e., to invent lyrics on the spot, based on single-word prompts. When the rappers freestyled, their default and executive networks showed the same pattern of heightened and diminished activity as in the jazz pianists.[10] Other research has shown that decreased activity in regions of the executive network correlates with enhanced openness to creative ideas more generally.[11]

These and other studies suggest that Schiller's process

9 Limb CJ, Braun AR. Neural substrates of spontaneous musical performance: an fMRI study of jazz improvisation. PLoS ONE. 2008; 3(2): e1679.

10 Liu S et al. Neural correlates of lyrical improvisation: an fMRI study of freestyle rap. Scientific Reports. 2012; 2: 834.

11 Mayseless N et al. Unleashing creativity: the role of left temporoparietal regions in evaluating and inhibiting the generation of creative ideas. Neuropsychologia. 2014; 64: 157–168.

for improvisational creativity, a key characteristic of wit, occurs in two phases. The first involves the spontaneous generation of novel connections among disparate things (e.g., linking two words that sound the same but have different meanings), a process largely mediated by the default network. The second involves the focused evaluation and assembly of those connections into a witty remark (e.g., a pun), a process largely mediated by the executive network.

Witty thinking seems to recruit a unique configuration of neural processes that engage in seemingly contradictory modes of thought: the spontaneous and the deliberate, the generative and the evaluative.

The spontaneous, generative stage of this process bears a striking resemblance to another neurological condition, the "over-inclusive thinking" and "flight of ideas" exhibited by individuals diag-nosed with milder forms of bipolar disorder.

During the manic phase of cyclothymia, a condition in which mood swings do not meet the more severe clinical criteria of full-blown bipolar disorder, individuals often engage in "flight of ideas," stream of consciousness speeches in which thoughts flow so fast and free as to be almost incomprehensible. Cognition in this condition is often characterized by over-inclusion, an inability to filter out illogical or irrelevant thoughts.

As with *Witzelsucht*, however, muted forms of flight of ideas and over-inclusive thinking may actually heighten a person's facility for making the quirky connections characteristic of wit.

Ando and colleagues performed a comparative study of stand-up comedians to explore whether the cognitive processes involved in humor production were similar to those in individuals diagnosed with bipolar disorder.[12] (Though humor and wit may be regarded as distinct phenomena, the mechanisms of joke and witticism production are similar enough for this study to serve as a proxy for a more direct examination of wit.)

The researchers asked a group of comedians and a control sample of actors to complete an online questionnaire measuring four personality traits. They then compared the scores with each other and with general population norms.

Comedians ranked significantly above norms on all four scales, with particularly high scores on measures of introverted anhedonia (a reduced ability to feel social and physical pleasure, including an avoidance of intimacy) and extroverted impulsiveness (a tendency toward antisocial behavior, often suggesting a lack of mood-related self-control), both of which are associated with individuals with bipolar disorder.

Comedians also ranked significantly above norms on measures of unusual experiences (belief in the paranormal and a tendency to experience perceptual aberrations) and cognitive disorganization (distractibility and difficulty in focusing thoughts), both of which are associated with individuals with "divergent" thinking patterns.

In divergent thinking, multiple ideas are rapidly generated in a nonlinear manner, while in "convergent" thinking fewer ideas are generated in a much more structured manner.[13] Divergent thinking is associated with the default network, while convergent

12 Ando V, Claridge G, Clark K. Psychotic traits in comedians. British Journal of Psychiatry. 2014; 204: 341–345.

13 Runco, MA. Divergent thinking. In: Runco MA, Pritzker SR, editors. Encyclopedia of creativity. Vol. 2. San Diego: Academic Press; 1999, pp. 103–108.

thinking is associated with the executive network.

The Ando team concluded that the manic aspects of bipolar disorder shared some important characteristics with comedic performance; namely, quick associative leaps, novel nonlinear combinations, and rapidly changing ideation typically linked with divergent thinking.

The improvised monologues of comedian and actor Robin Williams, who was diagnosed with the neurodegenerative disorder Lewy body disease after his death by suicide in 2014,[14] demonstrate an extraordinarily high degree of divergent thinking. His last appearance on *The Tonight Show Starring Johnny Carson*, on May 21, 1992, is a particularly illustrative case in point.

Williams enters the stage with a rocking chair, the rockers of which are shaped like electric guitars, a gift he says he brought for Carson from "the Elvis estate." Williams makes his first malapropism— "Please, just sit on down and we'll give you a piña colonic"—within seconds.

Williams commits an Archie Bunkerism shortly thereafter, adopting the voice of a character who transposes the name of boxing promoter Don King with Rodney King, an African-American man who was severely beaten by Los Angeles police after a high-speed chase in March of the previous year. A few weeks before Williams's *Tonight Show* appearance, a mostly white jury acquitted the officers involved of assault, after which riots erupted in Los Angeles.

Many of Williams's remarks on the program alluded to the rioting, including a reference to then–vice president Dan Quayle, who just two days before the *Tonight Show* episode gave a

14 Schneider Williams S. The terrorist inside my husband's brain. Neurology. September 2016; 87(13): 1308–1311.

speech in which he claimed the rioting was "directly related to the breakdown of the family structure, personal responsibility and social order in too many areas of our society." In his speech, Quayle linked the unrest to what he deemed poor role models, singling out Murphy Brown, the divorced forty-something news anchor of the eponymous CBS sitcom who parented a child outside marriage.

Williams imagines a scenario in which Quayle, whom Williams describes as "one taco short of a combination plate," was initially instructed to talk about former California governor Jerry Brown but through a series of malapropic associations instead ends up talking about the sitcom mom Murphy Brown.

Assuming the character of Quayle, Williams begins chanting "Jerry Brown, Jerry Brown." Then, in a textbook demonstration of flight of ideas, he flits from Jerry Brown to Buster Brown (a mischievous little boy popular in the 1940s and '50s on TV and radio and also a brand of children's shoes), from Buster Brown to Audie Murphy (a World War II hero and film star of the 1940s and '50s), and finally from Audie Murphy to Murphy Brown.

Williams's riff is an amazing display of flight of ideas and over-inclusive thinking. Thought proceeds in wide associative patterns; ideas are generated very rapidly; focus shifts from moment to moment based on (sometimes distant) associations and wordplay. Unlike those suffering from pathology, however, Williams manages to steer his runaway train of thought to a relevant destination.

And, for audiences, arrival at that destination means keeping pace with Robin Williams's fleet-footed flights of ideas, a process that requires continuous and rapid incongruity detection and resolution and that enlists brain regions involved with the experience of mirth and reward.[15]

To follow the trajectory from Jerry Brown to Murphy Brown, listeners must simultaneously be aware of and apply knowledge from normally separate domains. Once relationships among these domains are resolved, listeners experience the mirth and reward characteristic of "getting" a pun or joke.[16] For example, the simultaneous awareness and application of knowledge from the domains of cuisine and comedy is necessary to resolve the incongruity in the question, "Why don't cannibals eat clowns?"[17]

Understanding a witty remark is therefore not unlike choosing the correct answer to a multiple-choice question,[18] for example:

> She had read so much about the harmful health effects of cigarettes that she decided to give up . . .
> A) Smoking
> B) Reading

Bihrle, Brownell, and Gardner developed the Joke and Story Completion Test (JSCT) to study humor generation and appreciation in brain-damaged patients.[19] In the JSCT, researchers present a joke stem with four possible endings: a non-humorous answer, a humorous non sequitur unrelated to the joke, a non-humorous non sequitur unrelated to the joke, and the witty ending:

---

15 Wyer Jr. RS, Collins II JE. A theory of humor elicitation. Psychological Review. 1992; 99(4): 663–688.

16 Brownell H et al. Surprise but not coherence: sensitivity to verbal humor in right-hemisphere patients. Brain and Language. 1983; 18(1): 20–27.

17 Because they taste funny.

18 Coulson S, Kutas M. Getting it: human event-related brain response to jokes in good and poor comprehenders. Neuroscience Letters. 2001; 316: 71–74.

19 Bihrle A, Brownell H, Gardner H. Comprehension of humorous and non-humorous materials by left- and right-brain damaged patients. Brain Cognition. 1986; 5(4): 399–411.

A visitor to Israel tours the Moscovitz Concert Hall and is impressed with the architecture and acoustics.[20] "Is this magnificent auditorium named after Chaim Moscovitz, the famous Talmudic scholar?" he inquires of the guide.

"No," the guide responds, "It is named after Sam Moscovitz, the writer."

"Never heard of him," the tourist says. "What did he write?"

The guide replies, "He wrote . . .

A) Towards A Neural Circuit Model of Verbal Humor Processing: An fMRI Study of The Neural Substrates of Incongruity Detection and Resolution

B) Your Mother's like a Railroad Track: Everybody Gets Laid

C) Apples Grow on Noses

D) A check

Choosing the "correct" ending to the joke requires resolving incongruities between associations with literature and associations with finance.

The opioid receptors responsible for feelings of mirth and reward are found in the greatest density in the association areas of the higher sensory cortices. Biederman and Vessel hypothesize that activation of cortical opioids might be the neural basis for the human motivation to seek out novel, richly ambiguous information—like puns, jokes, as well as witticisms—since resolution of those incongruous stimuli results in greater opioid release.[21] Therefore, the pleasure experienced when

20 Joke adapted from Marjorie Gottlieb Wolfe's The Schmooze site.

21 Biederman I, Vessel EA. Perceptual pleasure and the brain. American Science. 2006; 94: 249–255.

making new connections among disparate concepts could be nature's way of wiring human minds for creative exploration.

Conclusion

Schiller's "watchers at the gates" theory of imaginative thought, combined with insights from the study of *Witzelsucht* and other expressions of improvised creativity, may offer a useful model for understanding the neurological mechanisms involved in the generation and appreciation of wit. Given that witty remarks seem to activate the brain's key reward and learning regions, an investigation into how witticisms are created and delivered is a promising direction for future research.

ACKNOWLEDGMENTS

THE QUOTE AT the beginning of this chapter comes from "At the Speed of Instinct: Choosing Together to Play and Stay Together," a performance and lecture by Wynton Marsalis at Sanders Theater, Cambridge, Massachusetts, on April 17, 2013. Some of the jokes, puns, and wisecracks in this chapter come from sources other than the research papers whose findings they are used to illustrate. The author reports no conflicts of interest in researching and writing this chapter. The author thanks Justin Junge for permission to audit his course "Perception and Imagination" during his 2011–2012 Nieman Fellowship at Harvard, and Shelley Carson for permission to do the same for "Creativity Research: Madmen, Geniuses, and Harvard Students." Justin Junge provided invaluable comments and suggestions on drafts of this chapter.

> Wit lies in recognizing the resemblance among
> things that differ and the difference among
> things that are alike.
>
> ANNE LOUISE GERMAINE
> DE STAËL-HOLSTEIN

PERFECT WITTY EXPRESSIONS AND HOW TO MAKE THEM

*Being an exploration of stratagems and tactics to
enhance verbal wit's excellence and further its practice,
conveyed in emulation of Joseph Addison's**
Spectator *essays*

G IVEN THAT NO modern author I know of has written pro-
fessedly upon the subject of wit, and those who have ven-
tured upon the topic treat of it almost exclusively as an offshoot
of the discipline of humor, and that, too, in tired comic citations
and general exclamatory flourishes that do not get at the gist of the
matter, I hope to perform an acceptable work if I endeavor here
to treat of wit more analytically, with more rigor and more zest,
and, I hope, in a manner not unsuited to its acute, elusive nature.

---

* Joseph Addison (1672–1719) was an English essayist, playwright, and cofounder
of the *Spectator*, a daily magazine published from 1711–1712 that promised "to
enliven morality with wit, and to temper wit with morality" and in which Addison
penned a series of essays on the nature of wit.

Since, as an ancient sage once said, "A subject that will not bear raillery is suspicious, and a jest that will not bear serious examination is false wit," I aspire to shed light on my theme as well as to make light of it, thereby undertaking that by the end of this brief essay readers will have found ideas entertained and enlightened in ways that both elevate the spirit and advance the understanding.

I trust hereby to avoid the just censure of those critics who would accuse me of analyzing wit in a style that does not emulate it, as one who, examining individual stones from some great cathedral, finds nothing very special to say about them.

Thus, with this view in mind, I offer my notions of verbal wit, its various modes and methodologics, as I think they may tend to its continued refinement and perfection.

In one of his charming essays in the *Spectator*, Mr. Addison has an admirable reflection on the difference between true and false wit, whereby he attempts to show the former is of greater excellence than the latter. "True wit consists in the resemblance of ideas," he states, "and false wit in the resemblance of words."

By Mr. Addison's definitions, Archbishop Whately's* widely acclaimed riddle

Why can't you starve in the desert?
Because you can eat the sand which is there.
Who brought the sandwiches there?
Noah sent Ham, and his descendants mustered and bred.

---

* Richard Whately (1787–1863), Archbishop of Dublin and *Witzelsucht* sufferer, was famed for his inventive puns, including, "Noah's ark was made of gopher wood, but Joan of Arc was Maid of Orleans."

is a specimen of false wit, a mere lexical coincidence, consisting solely in the resemblance of words, there being no pertinent intellectual relation between cold cuts, condiments, and the Old Testament story of Noah's progeny.

In contrast, in Mr. Carlin's* observation

Atheism is a non-prophet institution

we find a most pertinent intellectual relation between atheism's lack of divinely inspired advocates and the influence and affluence of the Roman Catholic Church, one of the richest institutions on earth and the faith in which Mr. Carlin himself did profit from instruction in boyhood.

The implied comparison—and apparent contradiction—between the poor regard in which the irreligious have so often been held and the wealth and power of an ecclesiastical hierarchy that professes poverty make this saying a specimen of true wit, since it clearly consists in the resemblance of ideas as well as of words, demonstrating, as Mr. Addison also observed, "Not only the resemblance but the opposition of ideas does very often produce wit."

Though we may quibble with Mr. Addison's "true" and "false" designations—my own view being that both are genuine (both aforementioned examples are, in fact, puns, a genre for which I have elsewhere expressed my admiration) and both are to be commended for forging connections between unlike things—he nevertheless touches the fundament upon which all perfect

---

* Of religion, American comedian George Carlin (1937–2008) once remarked that he was not atheist or agnostic but acrostic: "The whole thing puzzles me."

witty expressions rest: resemblance, through concord or contrast, among thoughts, ideas, images, or objects.

Mr. Locke* arrived at a similar point when he sought to distinguish wit from judgment and to explain why a person generously endowed with the former might be sorely deficient in the latter. In this, Mr. Locke, like so many of his contemporaries, equated wit with the pleasant but misleading imprecisions of fancy, disdaining it in favor of the supposed superior intellection and seeming clearness of reason.

Judgment, Mr. Locke averred, lies in carefully separating one thing from another, a sundering that, he argued, assures escape from the siren song of similitude, whereby so many have been deluded into logical or moral error, fooled by false affinities.

With wit, the case is quite the opposite. Wit thrives in combination, not in isolation, and, as Mr. Locke correctly notes, lies "most in the assemblage of ideas, and putting those together with quickness and variety."

Mr. Lennon's quickness and variety were amply on display when, asked by a British reporter after the Beatles' 1964 U.S. tour how he found America, he answered, "Turn left at Greenland."

Ms. Parker employed the same device in response to the gentleman who, while pouring a cocktail, asked her to "Say when"; to which she replied, "Right after this drink."†

The wit in both cases turns on the alacrity with which the speakers observe resemblances—between the parallel meanings

---

* English philosopher John Locke (1632–1704) pitted wit against judgment in his *Essay Concerning Human Understanding.*

† Dorothy Parker (1893–1967) did not make this remark but, when writing footnotes, I am impelled to source an epigram, I sometimes cannot place the credit, so just assume Dorothy said it.

of "find" ("to experience" and "to locate") and the twin implica-
tions of "when" ("to dispense the libation" and "to commence
the flirtation")—and with which they assemble and inject those
observations into conversation.

Mr. Addison further discerned that not every quip should be
rightfully considered wit, but only those that affect the hearer
with surprise and delight. To assemble ideas with quickness and
variety requires little acuity if their resemblance is plainly manifest or already so often remarked as to be commonplace. There is
but slender wit in the poet's observation that his lover's breast is as
white as snow. Yet when he adds, forlornly, that it is also as cold,
a little wit slips in.

To create these effects, Mr. Addison concluded, "It is necessary
that the ideas should not lie too near one another in the nature
of things; for where the likeness is obvious, it gives no surprise."

None is more adept in how this is done than our esteemed
dean of St. Paul's Cathedral.* In "The Will," his elegy to unre-
quited love, he compares his spurned affections to a catalogue of
cherished possessions he bequeaths to those who have least want
or need of them—to ambassadors, whose constant occupation is
listening, his ears; to the sea, already surfeited with salt, his tears.

In the final stanza, he vows that when he gives up his last pos-
session, his life, love itself, will also cease to be, and

> Then all your beauties will be no more worth
> Than gold in mines, where none doth draw it forth;
> And all your graces no more use shall have,
> Than a sun-dial in a grave.

---

* The English metaphysical poet John Donne (1572–1631).

The image of "a sun-dial in a grave" surprises because the ideas so deftly here assembled lie not too near one another as to be obvious—on the contrary, the pairing of two items so rarely considered together is rather astonishing—yet they lie not so far apart as to be completely implausible. The image delights because the mind is drawn to a fresh perception by the combination of two things so starkly opposed yet nevertheless, in this fraught context, so startlingly apt.

If, then, wit consists, as we say, in binding together remote and separate notions, finding similarity in dissimilar things (or dissimilarity in similar things) and drawing the mind not only from one word to another but from one idea to another, then this is exactly the function of metaphor, which Mr. Tesauro* lauds as the "great mother of all witty expressions."

I have treated of metaphor at some length in another work, and will not repeat those arguments here, but do wish to briefly revisit the subject in order that metaphor's kinship with wit be more clearly delineated and its constitutive role in creative thought be more widely extolled.

More than any other thinker, save perhaps Aristotle himself, his exalted tutor and exemplar, Mr. Tesauro is wit's most passionate evangelist, proclaiming metaphor as the faculty of mind that takes thoughts, ideas, images, and objects and "connects or divides them, increases or diminishes them, deduces one from the other, indicates one by the other, and with marvelous dexterity replaces one with another, as jugglers do with objects . . . Whoever can recognize and join together such distant circumstances is more witty."

* Italian author Emanuele Tesauro (1592–1675) wrote a masterful treatise on metaphor called *The Aristotelian Telescope*.

Mr. Tesauro identifies three instrumental qualities of metaphor as they pertain to the composition of witty expressions—brevity, novelty, and clarity—and these I shall proceed to deal with, each in turn, using for illustrative purposes that most perfect of Mr. Lec's* many witty expressions:

No snowflake in an avalanche ever feels responsible.

Metaphor, Mr. Tesauro writes, "packs the objects tightly together in a single word and almost miraculously allows you to see one inside the other." This peculiar process of condensation explains why Mr. Lec's sentence, and, indeed, all witty expressions, can be so short yet so full of import: metaphor compresses a multitude of meaning into an exceedingly confined space.

One of the most miraculous aspects of Mr. Lec's saying is that, when understood literally, it signifies precisely nothing. How, one is compelled to ask, can a snowflake feel anything, much less responsibility? And responsibility for what, exactly? There is nothing in the literal meaning of the sentence as a whole, nor in any of its constituent parts, to even remotely suggest what the ultimate significance might be.

Yet, when examined through the lens of metaphor, we clearly see that Mr. Lec tightly packs multiple objects into the single word "avalanche," including the image of snowflakes as people and the inexorable force of opinion to which a lone voice may be subject when the desire for consensus and pressure for conformity quash potential dissent while simultaneously absolving individual members within a group of culpability for collectively

* The Polish aphorist Stanislaw Jerzy Lec (1909–1966).

made decisions. Despite its manifest complexity, this story effortlessly unfolds not so much on the page itself, but in the mind of the reader.

The stories told by metaphor are, however, Mr. Tesauro adds, "sketched rather than finished, so that ingenuity understands more than the tongue speaks." Perfect witty expressions must necessarily be incomplete, just as the greatest painters are able to depict the most expressive faces with a few simple brushstrokes and flourishes. This is due, in part, to the speed of their execution and, in part, because so much of their delight lies in the satisfaction listeners derive from deciphering them, using their own wits to deduce what is really meant from what is merely said.

Here, too, Mr. Lec proves himself a master of the form, since his saying barely even begins to suggest the vaguest outlines of its substance. He implies rather than asserts, hints rather than harangues, leaving his audience to shade in nuances of feeling as their experience and humors dictate.

The perfect witty expression can include so much because it leaves so much out.

In this way, metaphor shows us one thing inside another—in Mr. Lec's case, an all too human drama inside an avalanche—much like those ambiguous figures, once so common in popular magazines, which display two things at once: the shape of a vase created by faces gazing at one another, or a young lady coyly turned from the viewer who is also a hunched, craggy old woman.

The second of the three instrumental qualities of metaphor is novelty, whereby, Mr. Tesauro writes, "One object rapturously illuminated by another shoots like a lightning bolt into your intellect, and the novelty causes marvel."

Here I am put in mind of Professor Lichtenberg's discovery, while experimenting with an electrophore, of the beautiful, branchlike patterns formed when high-voltage electricity is discharged onto a surface covered in dust or sprinkled with various powders. By pressing blank sheets of paper onto the channels carved by the electrical bursts, or by directing the current through an insulating material on which the intricate folds are incised, these images, which the great German scientist described as "very glittering little twigs . . . similar to those which frozen moisture produces on glass window panes," may be recorded and preserved.

A metaphor, trapped, as it were, in the amber of a perfect witty expression, strikes me as very much akin to one of Professor Lichtenberg's electrical figures. The metaphor illumines in a flash each fork and foliation of a situation too complex or vexed to be otherwise immediately grasped, leaving every tributary traced, every ramification reified. The novelty of the representation etches a lasting impression, marking on the mind a bright trail of associations and insights, while also occasioning the surprise and delight of which Mr. Addison spoke as so essential to verbal wit.

The light cast by a brilliant image thus provides the third and final of metaphor's instrumental qualities—clarity.

This is why Mr. Locke is so grievously mistaken to disparage wit and separate judgment from it, for, in fact, metaphor increases understanding rather than diminishes it, by revealing intricacies of emotion and argument inaccessible to the broader, blunter instrument of reason. The perfect witty expression is no mere rhetorical flourish, but, as Mr. Tesauro rightly attests, an ingenious response to the "desire of human minds to learn new things effortlessly and many things briefly . . . This is the fast and easy teaching which produces pleasure, for the mind of whoever listens seems to hear an entire theatre of marvels in a single word."

In concluding these brief remarks on "the most perfect witty expressions and how to make them," to use Mr. Tesauro's phrase, I hope to have offered a glimpse behind the scenes of wit, where its ropes and pulleys and other theatrical machinery may be studied up close and in operation, and to have adequately acquitted myself of my original purpose in treating of this theme: to lay out the elements of which perfect witty expressions consist—namely, the detection, through concord or contrast, of resemblances, and the adroit assembly of such resemblances into brief, novel, and clear metaphorical statements, combining images lying not too far apart from one another, yet also not too near, and affecting the hearer with the emotions of surprise and delight.

In this I hope to have provided sufficient examples and sure evidence of Mr. Tesauro's contention that through wit "mute things speak, the insensible live, the dead revive . . . So only those things that are not vivified by wit are truly dead."

I shall have more to say on verbal wit and the sparkling conversational embellishments so central to it, as well as on other varieties of witty experience, including the practical, the innovative, the observational, the visual, and the spiritual, in the pages that follow, should I be granted the favor of your continued attention.

Jive is language in motion.

DAN BURLEY

Advanced Banter

Being a primer on the wit of jive and its related
rhetorical forms, beginning with a section composed
in jive of the 1930s and '40s and concluding
with a glossary of terms from the great practitioners

Dig that dipper for some brine, Jackson, and cool
your heels a tick while I boot you to this deuce of cats who long
ago trilled, laying down a line of solid jive fine as French wine and
hard as Norwegian lard. Just stash your frame on that soft top and
lay a light splash of spray on me, and I'll cool you and school you in
some mellow banter guaranteed to carve your knob.

Ole Dan Burley was a well-hipped stud from Lexington, land
of the long white rolls and giggle water, who came to the south
side of the City of the Big Wind, where he copped dead presidents
scribbling for a snitchpad.

As a lean green teen, strictly the lick and most fly but still dripping behind the flaps, Burley started wiggling his fishhooks on the
elephant teeth at "rent parties." That's where, during the Big Bad
Blue, skint cats weeded the saw by decking out their cribs as glad
pads where the colts and the fillies, all draped in their mad fronts,

could line their flues, guzzle foam, slice their chops, and cut the rug for just a few brown Abes and buffalo heads.

There, frisking his whiskers on those rickety 88s, did our man, Dapper Dan, most directly and correctly wake the world to that crazy beat called "skiffle."

Roundabout that same chime, there was another kitty just as witty, Lavada Durst, and he, too, lashed his paddles on the goola to much mitt pounding from the hipsters and the hustlers at rent parties. Durst's clambakes went down in Austin, land of cow town barrelhouses and sky-high chimneys for the conkpiece, where he burped out the chirps over the ether before wheeling righteous spiels and falling to his prayer bones for the Head Knock every seven brights over at the Olivet Baptist Church.

Ole Lavada anointed himself "Dr. Hepcat" because his mugging was so cunning and his riffing so tripping.

Burley and Durst spread this hard mess by scratching out jive bibles on their desk pianos, wherein the hep and the unhep alike could pad their knowledge boxes with the finest pulp about laying down solid signifying and deepest sugar. Click your gimmers on these scrolls, Jelly Roll, and you'll be woofin' fine as home cookin', like Tip Toe Joe strictly in the know, like the tree all root, like the letter all wrote, like the road all rut, and I mean truly in the groove.

Trig your wig to this jig scribbled by Burley the squares and gators pule by the sparkside every Yule:

'Twas the dim before Nicktide, and all through the crib,
You could hear Joe Hipp spieling that righteous ad lib.
Them leg-sacks were stashed by the smoke-hole, in fact,
They were a Lamb's unhipped beg on Santa's fine sack;
The cats and the chippies were all knocking a nod,
While the most anxious ideas through their thinkboxes trod;

And the Head Chick was snorting, but I tossed and rolled,
Trying to collar a wink, as Hawkins blew cold;
"Let your gimmers pop open," loudly cried Joe Hipp,
I bounced from my softy, gave the lilies a flip,
Trillied to the glass-gazer to dig the outside;
And in the heavy pitch black, overhead I spied,
The pumpkin riding gently, and grinning so fine,
It was digging its kicks from the gleaming snow-shine.

Snap your cap to Durst's Broadway squawk chipped off the dome of ole Joe Addison, that eighteenth century icky from the layout across the drink:

I stash me down to cop a nod.
I put my mellow frame upon the sod.
If I should cop a drill before the early toot
I'll lay a spill on the head knock to make everything allroot.
So with that, fly cat, I'll chill my chat
and fall back to my righteous pad and cop a nod like mad.

You best turn your lamps up full bright, Dwight, because this jive is no joke but the surest cure for sorest hypes. When the lip-splitters, sweet-hissers, baby-kissers, and all their fraughty issue would make you scarf onions, slide your jib to the light side of the stroll and get some traction on that action. Do no wrong with your boots on.

I'm going to take a powder out of this house of countless drops and ooze on down to the reading and writing rockpile, for my rug needs much dusting. Latch on to the knowledge I'm dropping and you'll be hip to the tip and most verily on the beam, from the rising of the bean to the going down of the same, when all manner of things will be copacetic and you will surely have it much made. Like the farmer said to the 'tater, I'll plant you now and dig you later.

•　　•　　•　　•　　•

"EVERYONE KNOWS THAT life isn't half as thrilling, as exciting, or as picturesque as it should be," Dan Burley wrote in his *Original Handbook of Harlem Jive*. "Jive undertakes to remedy that situation with language that makes up for the dullness of mere existence."

Jive, the form in which the above monologue is written (for assistance in understanding the text, see the glossary of jive terminology included below), was invented by African-American jazz musicians in the 1920s, '30s, and '40s. The term might derive from several words in African languages—possibly from the Wolof *jev*, "to verbally disparage," or the Efik-Ejagham *jiwe*, which means "monkey" and refers to the Signifying Monkey, an African folkloric figure known for his trickery and clever use of language. "Jive" might also be related to the English word "gibe"—to taunt, scoff, or mock. During the first half of the twentieth century, Dan Burley and Lavada Durst were among the great practitioners—and great popularizers—of the form.

Burley, born in 1907 in Lexington, Kentucky, worked as a sports correspondent, general reporter, and gossip columnist in Chicago, often writing his column "Back Door Stuff," in jive. He was also an accomplished pianist, performing with jazz legends like Lionel Hampton and Dizzy Gillespie.

Burley intended his *Original Handbook of Harlem Jive*, published in 1944, "to give students of Jive . . . an idea of what it is all about." In addition to providing a glossary and a brief history of the form, Burley included folktales, excerpts from Shakespeare's plays, and poems, like Clement Clarke Moore's "A Visit from St. Nicholas" quoted above, reworked in jive.

Lavada Durst, born in 1913 in Austin, Texas, was also an accomplished pianist, specializing in barrelhouse, a combination of blues and ragtime. He worked part-time as a disc jockey, talking in jive while introducing records, calling baseball games, and making public service announcements. He eventually became a minister and in 1953 self-published *The Jives of Dr. Hepcat*, which also included a glossary and a selection of familiar texts, like the bedtime prayer quoted above, rendered in jive.

For Burley, Durst, and the other African-Americans who developed and codified jive, the language may well have been a way to make up "for the dullness of mere existence," as Burley put it. But it was also more than a mere conversational diversion.

Jive was a declaration of linguistic independence, a form of discourse separate from and inaccessible to the dominant white culture. It parodied, with power and panache, formal types of speech, while creating a wholly original idiom rich in memorable imagery and metaphorical expression. According to Mezz Mezzrow, a white jazz clarinetist, saxophonist, and contemporary of Burley and Durst, jive was "a satire on the conventional ofay's [white person's] gift of gab and gibberish . . . [Jive] was more than a secret code; it was jammed with a fine sense of the ridiculous that had behind it some solid social criticism."

Jive was also a declaration of linguistic combat, a contest rooted, in part, in stories about the battles between the Signifying Monkey and the Lion. In the folktales of the Yoruba people of Nigeria and Benin, the Lion continually oppresses the Signifying Monkey, and the Signifying Monkey continually escapes this oppression by outwitting the Lion through cunning use of language. In one famous account of the rivalry, the Signifying Monkey lures the Lion into a fight with the Elephant by claiming, falsely, that the Elephant has been insulting the Lion's family:

> The Monkey and the Lion got to talkin' one day.
> Monkey say, "There's a bad cat [the Elephant]
> livin' down your way . . .
> He say folks say you king,
> and that may be true,
> But that he can whip the daylights out of you.
> And somethin' else I forgot to say:
> He talks about your mother
> in a hell of a way."

Enraged, the Lion sets out to exact revenge on the Elephant. In the ensuing battle, the Elephant easily trounces the Lion.

The Signifying Monkey was regarded as such a role model, and his verbal facility was so highly valued, that the jive term for speaking in a clever or witty—though not necessarily truthful—way is "signifying."

"The idea right smack in the middle of every cat's mind all the time was this: He had to sharpen his wits every way he could, make himself smarter and keener, better able to handle himself, more hip," Mezzrow wrote of jive and its Harlem practitioners in his autobiography *Really the Blues*. "On The Corner the idea of a kind of mutual needling held sway, each guy spurring the other guy on to think faster and be more nimble-witted . . . They spouted at each other like soldiers sharpening their bayonets—what they were sharpening, in all this verbal horseplay, was their wits, the only weapons they had."

Just as jazz improvises responses to what others play, jive improvises responses to what others say.

Games of combative banter like this have a long history in many different cultures. In medieval Spain, wandering scholar-minstrels amused themselves during travel by berating one another—in Latin, of course. At the Souk Okaz in Saudi Arabia, the site of poetry competitions since pre-Islamic times, rival bards recite poems praising their own tribes and dissing others. The Scots enjoyed "flyting," bouts of intense and usually obscene verbal jousting; the Nigerians perfected a theatrical exchange of abuse known as *Ikocha Nkocha*, or "the making of disparaging remarks"; and the Japanese refined *haikai*, the contentious composition of linked stanzas that often took a satiric or vulgar tone.

The Dozens, a form of interactive insult whose name may come from an old English verb meaning "to stun or stupefy," is part of the African-American tradition of competitive verbal invention. In the Dozens, combatants face off before a crowd and direct aspersions at their adversary's shortcomings, which typically include lack of intelligence, unfortunate physical appearance, inferior social status, dire pecuniary circumstances, regrettable hygienic standards, and absence of sexual experience, not to mention the questionable morality of various family members, especially mothers and grandmothers.

A typical opening gambit might be,

Your mother's like a doorknob—everybody gets a turn.

To which the second player might respond,

Your mother's like a cake—everybody gets a piece.

From there, the rivals might progress to a consideration of comparative intellectual abilities, with the first player opining,

> You're so dumb it takes you an hour-and-a-half to watch *60 Minutes*.

To which the second player might reply,

> You're so dumb you think the Supreme Court is where Diana Ross plays tennis.

The ultimate goal of the Dozens is to exceed or eclipse your opponent with the sass and savvy of your one-liners. Contestants exchange this kind of smack talk until the audience indicates a winner by the volume of their applause.

"I learned to talk in the street, not from reading about Dick and Jane going to the zoo and all that simple shit," H. Rap Brown (known as Jamil Abdullah Al-Amin after his conversion to Islam), a controversial civil rights activist and early practitioner of what eventually became rap, recounts in his autobiography. "We played the Dozens for recreation, like white folks played Scrabble."

Like jive, though, the Dozens is more than just a game. Persuasion is an important means of achieving status within a group, whether that group happens to find itself on a Harlem street corner or the floor of the Senate. And Dozens encounters aren't won by abuse alone but by goading, coaxing, cajoling, convincing, and generally getting your way with words.

In this, the Dozens is a contemporary take on the ancient art of sophistry. The Sophists, a loose group of itinerant Greek scholars, taught young statesmen how to wield language in ways that would amuse, instruct, dissuade, and sway. Their interest was not so much in defending specific moral or political arguments, but in being able to defend *any* argument. Sophists sought virtuosity—regardless of the inherent virtue, or lack thereof, in their opinions.

Sophistic training consisted of continual linguistic play, with the goal of cultivating in students an ability to exploit logical or psychological openings during debate or disputation. Socrates used many of the Sophists' methods, and the taut give-and-take of his questioning method is also found in the Dozens, though in the Dozens the dialogue inevitably turns from Socratic to sarcastic.

This kind of caustic, improvisational wit is seldom welcomed by society at large. In Elizabethan England, all improvisation was banned from public performances. Actors were not permitted to deviate in any way from the letter of a text, and theater proprietors were forbidden to "suffer to be interlaced, added, mingled or uttered in any such play, interlude, comedy, tragedy or show any other matter than such as shall be first perused and allowed." The government feared extemporaneous entertainment might create space for unauthorized thought, and thus incite the populace to sedition.

One actor, however, was given special dispensation: Richard Tarlton, the most gifted clown of his day and the person many believe Shakespeare had in mind when he has Hamlet describe the dead court jester Yorick as "a fellow of infinite jest, of most excellent fancy." Tarlton died in 1588, about a decade before *Hamlet* was written.

Tarlton was beloved for his stage antics, which included an impressive repertoire of jigs, a gift for sarcastic raillery, and an uncanny ability to improvise rhymes. After the curtain fell on a performance, Tarlton often reappeared onstage and challenged the audience to call out clever couplets, to which he would instantly reply in kind. The exchanges could become aggressive, but he was so good at it that the practice of ad-libbing witty verse came to be known as "tarltonizing."

Once, when an audience member shouted a couplet implying that Tarlton was insufficiently independent of his wife,

> Methinks it is a thing unfit
> To see a gridiron turn the spit

his swift rejoinder was,

> Methinks it is a thing unfit
> To see an ass have any wit.

Tarlton's exploits were the Dozens skirmishes of his time, not unlike the "cutting contests"—impromptu competitions among musicians to see who could musically outdo whom—that took place at the improvised apartment concerts, or "rent parties," at which Burley and Durst performed.

In a cutting contest, one player begins by introducing a tune, then the other players cut in—picking up and changing the melody, introducing different keys or beats, and generally attempting to excel in inventiveness every other musician in the room. The practice is still alive, in more collaborative form, in the jazz tradition of trading solos and, in verbal displays, at rap battles, where rappers vie to extemporize the most original disses and the best rhymes.

If wit is, as Aristotle defined it, "educated insolence," then jive and the Dozens—and their contemporary descendants, rap and hip-hop—are its classic rhetorical expressions.

Glossary of Jive, Derived from The Great Practitioners

A

Allroot: Alright

B

Banter: Witty repartee

Bean: The sun

Big Bad Blue: The Great Depression

Boot: To describe, explain, inform

Boots on: Capable

Broadway squawk: Prayer (Broadway: Heaven, the best; Squawk: Exclamation)

Brown Abes and buffalo heads: Small change

Burp out the chirps: Sing, play, or broadcast music

C

Carve your knob: Entertain or enlighten (Knob: Head)

Cat: A cool, witty person. From the Wolof word *katt*, the hereditary caste of singers who kept the oral history of the tribe

Chill: Stop, cease

Chime: Time

Chimneys for the conkpiece: Hats (Conkpiece: Head)

Chippies: Young women

Clambake: Jam session

Collar: To get, grab

Collar a wink: Sleep

Colts and fillies: Young men and women

Cool your heels: Wait, hang out

Cop: To take, understand

Cop a nod: Sleep

Cop a drear: Have something bad happen to you

Copacetic: Excellent, the best, tops

Cow town barrelhouses: Disreputable bars

Crib: House, apartment, room

Cut the rug: To dance

D

Dead presidents: Paper money

Deep sugar: Sweet talk

Desk piano: Typewriter

Deuce: Two

Dig: To conceive, perceive,

think. From the Wolof *deg* or *dega*, to "understand" or "appreciate"

Dig that dipper for some brine: Ask the bartender for a drink

Dome: Head, brain

Drape: To dress

Drink: Ocean

Dripping behind the flaps: Wet behind the ears

E

Early bright: Morning

Eighty-eight (88): Piano

Elephant teeth: Piano keys

Every seven brights: Once a week

F

Fish hooks: Fingers

Fly: On the ball, smart

Fraughty issue: Bad situation

Frisk the whiskers: To warm up before a gig

Fronts: Clothes

G

Giggle water: Alcohol

Gimmers: Eyes

Glad pad: Party spot

Glass-gazer: Window

Goola: Piano

Guzzle foam: To drink beer

H

Hard: Fine, excellent

Hawkins: Wind (from jazz saxophonist Coleman Hawkins)

Head Knock: God

Hep: To be alert, to think on one's feet. From the Wolof *hipi*, "awareness" or "acuity"

Hepcat: Smart, clever person. From the combination of the Wolof *hipi* ("aware") and *katt* ("singer")

Homey: Friend

House of countless drops: Bar

Hype: Plot, scheme, swindle

I

Icky: Conservative person

J

Joe Addison: Joseph Addison, eighteenth century English essayist who wrote a version of the bedtime prayer quoted in this chapter

K

Knowledge box: Brain

L

Lamb: A sucker, an easy mark
Lame: Incapable, failed
Lamps: Eyes
Latch on: To understand
Layout: Place
Leg-sacks: Stockings, socks
Light splash of spray: A glass of water
Lilies: Bedsheets
Line the flue: To eat
Long ago trilled: Lived in the past
Long white rolls: Cigarettes

M

Mad: To feel good, look fine
Mellow: Fine, excellent, superior
Mess: Something fun or exciting
Mitt pounding: Applause

O

On the beam: Smart, knowing, in the groove
Ooze: To move, walk

P

Paddles: Hands
Prayer bones: Knees
Pulp: Information

R

Riff: Musical or verbal passage
Righteous: Superlative, incomparable
Rockpile: Building
Rug: Head

S

Scarf onions: To be made to do or experience something unpleasant (Scarf: To eat)
Signify: To speak wittily
Skiffle: A musical mixture of jazz, blues, and folk
Skint: Penniless
Skull orchard: Graveyard
Slice the chops: To chatter
Slide your jib: To speak fluently
Smoke-hole: Chimney
Snap your cap: To pay attention to
Snitchpad: Newspaper
Softy: Bed
Solid: Wonderful, excellent
Sparkside: Fireside

Spiel: Oration, narration, dissertation

Squares and gators: Uncool people and music fans

Stash: To put or place

Stash your frame: Sit or lie down

Stem: Street, avenue

Strictly the lick: Very nice, fine

Stroll: Street, avenue

T

Take a powder: Depart

Thinkbox: Brain

Tick: A short period

Trig your wig: To pay attention to (Wig: Head)

Trilly: To go

W

Wake: To bring to the attention of

Weed the saw: Pay the rent (Weed: To give; Saw: Landlady)

Well-hipped stud: Man in the know

Woofin': To speak wittily, signify

AN ODE TO WIT

Being a paean to wit, rendered in rap

Tell me, O tell, what kind of thing is wit?
Is it the summit of punditry? Or is it just talking shit?
If poetry (O woe is me!) is the best words in their best order,
Witticisms—I don't mean criticism—are the
best turds in their best ordure.

Wit. It's the shit. Wit. It's so lit.

Wit glories in stories, in soaring oratory.
Like Cowley, it wows me, endows me with ingenious allegories.
Wit floors me, restores me, and then it implores me:
"Iamb who am. Thou shalt have no other gods before me."

Wit's the showboat of gnosis, the ringmaster of rhetoric,
A brainteaser, crowd pleaser, spitting licks you don't expect.
Look behind the punch line and you'll
find it going 'bout its business:
Jokes can be private, bro, but wit needs witnesses.

Wit leaps then looks. Please read my book.

Now you're asking me, "Hey, what's a metaphor?"
Oh, say, can't you see what it's aiding and abetting for?
You got some ideas, thoughts you want to polish?
You don't need a college to drop this kind of knowledge.

Find your subject, go public, and let your thoughts obtrude
By composing, proposing an apt similitude.
Use images—they're limitless—all you can beg, steal, or borrow,
Just like Lin-Manuel Miranda and Emanuele Tesauro.

Make it immediate, take these ingredients,
and stir them in the pot.
Match them, mix them, watch the plot thickening.
Then step back, unpack, and let readers connect the dots:
That's how you tell it like it is by saying what it's not.

Cut to the quick. Wit. Make it sick.

Hey yo, metis is my fetish.
It's what keeps me compos mentis.
If you neglect it you'll regret it,
So to keep your wits best don't forget this:

When things seem senseless, when you're defenseless,
Be just as cunning as old Master K'ung-ming.
Open the throttle. Go get your bottle.
Say the secret woid and win an extra sixty dollahs!

If you're in trouble learn to juggle

So when the flood comes your head's above it.

Be resourceful. Be remorseless.

See the trees despite the forest.

Read my lips. Shoot from the hip.

Wit switch hits. Wit ad-libs. It teaches new dogs lotsa old tricks.

Throw spaghetti 'gainst the wall—wit's what sticks.

You can't beat it or repeat it, not even with a shtick.

Wit rocks the boat. That's all she wrote.

Turn it and turn it, for everything is in it.

Reflect on it and grow old

and gray with it. Don't turn from it,

for nothing is better than it.

BEN BAG BAG, *PIRKE AVOT*

TURNING WORDS

*In which the author reprises aspects of wit already
addressed and prefigures those yet to come*

1

"TIME FLIES LIKE an arrow; fruit flies like a banana." This quip is an instance of syntactic ambiguity, which occurs whenever a verbal unit gives rise to multiple, more or less equally valid interpretations. This particular saying is also known as a "garden path sentence," a grammatically correct text that begins with what seems like a single, fairly obvious meaning but then unexpectedly shifts to a completely different meaning, thereby luring readers down one interpretative track only to suddenly shunt them onto quite another one. To be led by a garden path sentence is to be misled. But there comes a point in every sentence, as on every garden path, at which the mind must take a turn, for better or for worse, deciding which direction to choose, which of all possible meanings to apply. In Japanese verse, the words or phrases from which these decisions emanate are called *kake-kotoba*, points at which poems pivot from predictability to surprise, points that appear as often in life as they do in literature. To Aristotle, the fleet-minded individual adept at gracefully, playfully executing and following these swerves has *eutrapelia*, being full of "good turns," which he considered a defining characteristic of wit.

2

BEFORE THE WIDESPREAD use of electricity, homes were lit by "illuminating gas" derived from coal. Horticulturists noticed that plants did poorly in greenhouses illuminated by this gas. Various inquiries from growers came to William Crocker and Lee Knight, researchers at the University of Chicago's botany laboratory, as to the effect of illuminating gas on the flowering carnation. Gas leaking from defective pipes caused the buds to close and go to sleep, never again to open, inflicting considerable financial loss. Crocker and Knight also observed that in private homes lit by illuminating gas, cut carnations lasted only a few hours before going to sleep. They identified one component of the gas—ethylene—as the source of this odd botanical sleeping sickness. Ethylene is a naturally occurring hydrocarbon gas that can be explosive in high concentrations. In fruit, ethylene is a ripening agent. The riper an apple, the more ethylene it emits. When apples are stored together, the ethylene each apple emits stimulates all the other apples to emit more ethylene, too. A single apple can thus stimulate all the apples around it to ripen faster and eventually rot. This is the origin of the saying, "One bad apple spoils the barrel."

3

MY UNCLE JACK stood well north of six feet tall. He was thin as a rake, with hair razed into a permanent burr. His veined and cratered nose was a topographic map of the moon. Chain-smoking Viceroys added a congested gurgle to his natural bass-baritone, which he regularly invoked from his perch on a vinyl-upholstered folding chair to shout down relatives and belt out "Daddy's Little

Girl" and other sentimental tunes. As kids, my cousins and I used to hide under the sofa during rowdy family gatherings and secretly tape-record the proceedings, which consisted of relentless roasting of various relatives and occasional skits and performances. After a few drinks, Uncle Jack's voice rose loud and clear above the racket, an unceasing source of recklessly definitive opinions and wildly off-key singing. Uncle Jack was the first of our aunts and uncles to pass away. At his viewing, my father stood at the door of the funeral parlor greeting people as they came in. Some of the younger cousins loitered awkwardly outside, unsure what to do or how to behave. "You better hurry up and get in there if you want to see Uncle Jack with his mouth shut," my father said.

4

DR. JOHNSON DID not approve. Of the metaphysical poets, a group of seventeenth century English writers he was the first to define and dismiss, Johnson argued their imagery was forced and their conceits—the ingenious extended metaphors they made linking dissimilar things—far-fetched. "The most heterogeneous ideas are yoked by violence together," Johnson railed. "Nature and art are ransacked for illustrations, comparisons, and allusions." John Donne, dean of London's St. Paul's Cathedral, was the most conceited metaphysical of all. In "Love's Progress," he contends that spurning carnal for platonic passion is like feeding meat to the stomach not through the mouth but through the rectum. Donne defends the "right true end" of love by overturning love poetry's conventional tropes. He deposes the beloved's face in favor of a foot fetish and grounds high-flown romantic rhetoric firmly in the groin. By establishing correspondences between apparently unlike things, conceits create surprising intellectual symmetries. Dr. Johnson's disfavor notwithstanding, and despite any lingering ifs, ands, or buts, it is through conceits that the mind both discovers and expresses new insights and ideas. The conceit is a compass that, however far one foot may roam, the other, fixed foot will always draw it back home.

5

AROUND THE MIDDLE of the seventeenth century, England's austere Puritan leaders began closing theaters and suppressing celebrations of Christmas and Easter. To make money, actors performed "drolls," short scenes from well-known plays to which they added bits of physical humor and merry dancing, creating what eventually became the comedy sketch. The word "droll" entered English via the French *drôle* (odd, comical, funny) and the Dutch *drol* (a goblin, "fat little fellow" or, via a visual metaphor, a turd or piece of excrement). Droll wit has always had an affinity with feces, a substance that contains within itself the fertile beginning and desiccated end of all things, that stuff in which the scatological and eschatological meet. Tenali Rama attended a royal feast at which the debate turned to life's greatest physical pleasure—eating or sex. Some of the gorged and intoxicated guests argued for eating; others argued for sex. Tenali Rama argued that defecation, not eating or sex, was life's greatest physical pleasure. The revelers, disgusted by this suggestion, drove Tenali Rama from the room. Outside, he locked the door and waited. Soon enough, guests banged on the door, clamoring for release. "Now what is life's greatest pleasure?" Tenali Rama asked.

6

FOR MILLENNIA, COMPETITIVE riddling has been a whetstone against which to sharpen wit. The Anang of Nigeria, whose tribal name means "having the ability to speak wittily yet meaningfully upon any occasion," pride themselves on their eloquence. Young people are trained from an early age in the art of public speaking, and riddles are an integral part of this education. Upon meeting an acquaintance, one person might ask, "What has two wings yet cannot fly?" "A roof," the other might reply. Proverbs are also used to prompt critical thinking and reinforce moral lessons. When met with the proverb, "A single vine does not fill a forest," a person might respond with, "A single coin that falls makes no sound." Both sayings stress the importance of cooperation and collaboration among kin. "Neck riddles," so called because giving the right answer can be a matter of life or death, present seemingly insoluble puzzles. When the Mogul emperor Akbar drew a line in the sand and challenged his courtiers to make the line shorter without erasing any part of it, no one knew what to do. Birbal, his court jester, casually drew a longer line above it; the emperor's line was now shorter.

7

ONE DAY AN old man lost his only horse. The old man was poor, and without his horse he could not properly tend his crops. All his neighbors in the village arrived to commiserate with the old man about his bad luck. "How do you know this is bad luck?" he asked. A few days later, the old man's horse returned, bringing with it a pack of wild horses, which the old man could tame and sell. All the neighbors arrived to congratulate the old man on his good luck. "How do you know this is good luck?" he asked. One day the old man's son fell off one of the wild horses while trying to tame it and broke his leg. The doctor said the old man's son would have a limp for the rest of his life. All the neighbors arrived to commiserate with the old man and his son about their bad luck. "How do you know this is bad luck?" the old man asked.

The next year, the emperor declared war on a rival kingdom, and all able-bodied young men were required to serve. Because of his bad leg, the old man's son was not drafted.

8

THE ANCIENT KOREAN poetic form sijo consists of three lines. The first line introduces the poem's idea or theme; the second line further develops that idea or theme; and the third line slips in a dramatic twist, a clever turn of phrase, plot, or thought. Yang Saon, a sixteenth century bureaucrat and avid mountain climber, wrote only one known sijo, about Mount Geumgangsan in what is now North Korea, but that poem has become part of Korean national lore, still memorized by every schoolchild:

> Men may say the mountain's high, but all of it's beneath the
> sky.
> There is no reason we may not climb, but usually we never try.
> We only say, "The mountain's high."

Sijo are syllogisms, in which neither the premises nor the conclusion are explicitly stated, with everything hinging on that third line, the point where the poem swivels, as in the following exercise in the form, composed for my daughter on her fourteenth birthday:

> My daughter, shirt too short, shorts too tight, slams the door,
> Dismissing my observation that spring's late this year and she
> might need a sweater:
> "Shut up, Dad. I can dress myself and you don't understand
> anything about my life anyway."

9

AFTER THE ALLIED D-Day landings in June 1944, German Lieutenant General Hermann B. von Ramcke holed up in Brest, at the western tip of Brittany in France, with forty thousand men. His orders were to hold the city, an important deepwater port for Nazi U-boats, as long as he could. Von Ramcke believed he faced General George S. Patton's Third Army, so he prepared for a long siege. In fact, Patton was already racing east toward Paris. Less than a thousand American troops, most from the secret "ghost army" unit, which spent the war impersonating more menacing divisions, opposed the Germans at Brest. To convince Von Ramcke he confronted a more formidable foe, the ghost army populated the outskirts of the city with inflatable tanks, which would gradually leak during the day and be reinflated at night. Ghost army personnel repeatedly circled into town, changing vehicles and uniforms in transit, to trick local spies into thinking a greater fighting force was present. Ghost army soldiers hung out in bars wearing fake insignia, talking about imaginary troop deployments. If Von Ramcke had broken out of Brest, he could have harried Patton from behind. Instead, he stayed put, surrendering on September 19.

10

TO EARN A London black cab license, drivers spend several years buzzing around town on a moped to acquire "The Knowledge," the ability to navigate the British capital from memory. This is challenging because London, which over hundreds of years evolved into a single city from separate villages, is laid out like a brain, with thousands of narrow, winding convolutions, whereas a place like Manhattan is laid out more like a computer chip, in a predictable grid with helpfully numbered streets. A cabbie who successfully masters "The Knowledge" has a larger hippocampus, a brain region involved in spatial navigation and long-term memory, than someone who fails the test or who never seeks to gain "The Knowledge" in the first place. Neuroplasticity is the brain's capacity to continually grow, change, and form new connections in response to fresh experiences and information. According to psychologist William James, two things are required to maintain the brain in plastic shape: attention and effort, both of which are also essential to wit. "Attention and effort are . . . but two names for the same psychic fact," James wrote in his essay "Habit." "Keep the faculty of effort alive in you by a little gratuitous exercise every day."

11

IN APRIL OF 1985, the crew members of the space shuttle *Discovery* successfully deployed a multimillion-dollar communications satellite—only to see it malfunction almost immediately, for one of the simplest, most infuriating reasons: the power switch refused to click on. Maneuvering the *Discovery* close enough to the satellite to effect repairs would have been too dangerous, but the team kept their wits about them, cobbling together what they called "the fly-swatter" from objects found around the ship— plastic covers torn from flight manuals, spare plastic plumbing tubes, an aluminum frame with a window shade. Using just scissors, a Swiss Army knife, and needle and thread from a space-suit repair kit, they cut rectangular holes in the flight manual covers, affixed these to a piece of plastic rolled into the shape of a cone, and attached this to an extendable rod constructed from the extra sections of plumbing tubes. They then connected this to the shuttle's robotic arm, which, with *Discovery* itself at a safe distance, they extended toward the satellite's stubborn power switch. After some trial and error, the crew managed to snag the switch in one of the flight manual covers' rectangular holes and flick it on. Mission accomplished.

12

AS BUSTER KEATON settles down on a bench to read his local daily, he unfolds the paper to standard broadsheet format. He soon notices, though, that the newspaper is bigger than he expected, so he continues unfolding it—first to roughly the surface area of an ample picnic blanket, then easily to the proportions of a king-sized sheet, until he's finally engulfed by a single gigantic swath of newsprint. Keaton's gags start innocuously enough, with some ordinary object, then snowball into astonishing displays of physical and visual wit. Keaton, a stockbroker on the verge of financial ruin, learns he will inherit handsomely from his grandfather—if he weds by seven p.m. When his sweetheart rebuffs him (she will marry for love, not for money), he places an open offer of marriage, with details of the pecuniary benefits, in the newspaper. Hundreds of women turn up at church for the ceremony, only to become enraged at Keaton's tactics. The bevy of would-be brides chases him out of town, onto a nearby hill, where he dislodges a single rock, which sets in motion an avalanche of boulders, which rain down on our hapless groom's head. Magnified by wit, the mundane becomes magnificent.

13

STROLLING BY A table where two men are playing a game of poker, Harpo Marx hears one man tell the other, "Cut the cards," whereupon he produces an ax and chops the deck in half. As stowaways on an ocean liner headed to America, Harpo and Chico elude the ship's onboard detectives by infiltrating the orchestra during a performance. Chico briefly picks out a tune on the grand piano and then abruptly flees, leaving Harpo to tinker with a few bars of Rachmaninoff as the cops lie in wait in the wings. Harpo plays for time, knowing his unexpected recital is the only thing staving off the long arm of the law. When he comes to the forte section of the piece, however, he pounds so hard on the piano that it starts to fly apart. One chord sends the lid spinning off; another splinters the keyboard into broken teeth; another cracks the frame into kindling. Rummaging through the wreckage, Harpo extracts the piano strings, still in their harplike triangular metal frame, which he cradles on his shoulder and begins to strum. "Wit lies in recognizing the resemblance among things that differ and the difference among things that are alike."

14

WHEN THE GOD Kareya created the world, he said to the human being, "Make as many bows and arrows as there are animals and give the longest to the animal that is to have the most power and the shortest to the animal that is to have the least." Every animal wanted to get the longest bow, so Coyote decided to stay up all night to be first in line when the bows were handed out in the morning. As the night wore on, Coyote became sleepier and sleepier. He tried to stay awake by walking around and jumping up and down. He sharpened two sticks to prop his eyelids open but soon fell asleep, the sticks piercing his eyelids and sealing them shut. In the morning, the cougar received the longest bow, and the frog received the next-to-last bow. Coyote was still asleep, and now only the shortest bow was left. "Who have I missed?" the human being asked. At that, Coyote awoke with a start, and all the other animals laughed. But the human being pitied Coyote and asked Kareya to give him more wit than all the other animals, even though he had received the shortest bow.

15

ONE NIGHT, AMID the alarms and excursions of yet another military campaign, K'ung-ming felt his mind clouding, his senses failing. The stars glowed clear. The battle flags hung motionless. The enemy that had so relentlessly pursued him and his bedraggled army seemed, for now, to have been eluded. The aged general retreated to his tent, informing his fretting lieutenants that should the flame of his lamp burn seven days he would live twelve months more, time enough to regain his strength, save the Han dynasty, and restore the glorious order that once was. Every day for the next six days, K'ung-ming remained silent and unseen inside his tent, meditating, planning troop movements, and spitting dark black blood into a bucket by his bed. His soldiers huddled around their miserable fires, muttering to themselves of fear and defeat, their eyes fixed on the general's tent for any sign of hope—or ruin. Each night K'ung-ming's lamp burned bright. His spirits rose, as did those of his men. On the evening of the seventh day, a young recruit rushed into K'ung-ming's tent with news of the enemy's approach, knocking over the general's lamp in his fright. Sometimes, wit works; sometimes, it doesn't.

16

HARPO'S FIRST IMPRESSION of Alexander Woollcott, the flamboyant, acerbic *New Yorker* theater critic, was of a plucked and over-inflated owl, with thick glasses and a mustache, dressed in an opera cape and a wide black hat, "like something that had gotten loose from Macy's Thanksgiving Day Parade." Their friendship began when Woollcott, smitten by the Marx Brothers' 1924 Broadway debut *I'll Say She Is*, barged into Harpo's dressing room after the show. Woollcott introduced Harpo to the group of authors, journalists, and playwrights who regularly lunched in the Rose Room of the Algonquin Hotel, where Harpo became the most taciturn member of the cadre of wisecracking wits known as the Algonquin Round Table. For years, Woollcott had no fixed abode, drifting from hotel to hotel, friend's apartment to friend's apartment, where his vitriolic, grandly delivered opinions made him a challenging houseguest. He eventually found his own place at the far end of East Fifty-second Street. Woollcott's fellow Round Tablers suggested a variety of ridiculous names for his new digs, with columnist Franklin P. Adams offering an invented Native American word, "Ocowoica," supposedly meaning, "The-Little-Apartment-on-the-East-River-That-It-Is-Difficult-to-Find-a-Taxicab-Near." But it was Dorothy Parker who came up with the name that eventually stuck: Wit's End.

The clown is the wit of action.

W. H. AUDEN

MY NAME
IS WIT

Being an examination of the Greek idea metis *as a model for those seeking to live by their wits, by means of a brief anthology of selected Trickster tales from various cultures*

Homer, like Saint Jerome and authors of other ancient epics, loved to make puns.

In the *Odyssey*, even the protagonist's name—Odysseus—is a pun. When our wandering hero's grandfather, Autolycus, famed in Greek lore for his sophistry and subterfuge, was asked to name his grandson, he said, "Because I got odium upon myself before coming here, odium from many, let the child's name be Odysseus to signify this."

Odysseus inherited his grandfather's gift for wordplay.

Arriving on the island of Cyclops, Odysseus discovers a cave filled with milk, cheese, and sheep. Through accomplished thievery, another skill he inherited from his grandfather, Odysseus could have made off with some mutton and dairy products. But, despite the misgivings of his men, he stays to explore the cave, lingering long enough to encounter its returning occupant, the one-eyed giant Polyphemus, who promptly devours two of his crew.

Having enjoyed these tasty morsels, and wanting to have more on hand for later, Polyphemus blocks the entrance to the cave with a boulder.

Odysseus and his men are trapped. Escape seems impossible. Odysseus can't simply kill Polyphemus, since the giant is the only one strong enough to remove the boulder. Instead, he decides to trick him.

Odysseus plies Polyphemus with drink until he is well and truly drunk. When the inebriated giant asks Odysseus his name, "No One" (*outis* in Greek) is the wily sailor's reply.

Polyphemus eventually passes out, and Odysseus plunges a red-hot staff into his eye. The blinded giant cries out for help—"'No One' is killing me! 'No One' is killing me!"—but none of his neighboring one-eyed giants come to help because they think he's just crazy drunk. Why call for help if no one is killing you?

The next morning, Polyphemus pushes aside the boulder just enough to let out his herd to graze, and Odysseus and his men flee by clinging to the bellies of the sheep as they exit.

When Odysseus tells Polyphemus his name, however, he does not use the word *outis*. He uses *metis*, another form of "no one" that puns on *metis*, a Greek philosophical term denoting the sly, crafty intelligence Odysseus displays throughout the *Odyssey*.

So, when Odysseus says, "My name is No One," what he's also saying is, "My name is Wit."

In Greek mythology, Metis was Zeus's first wife, goddess of wisdom and cunning. Her name gradually came to be used to describe anyone who deploys ingenuity, resilience, and deceit to overcome adversity. *Metis* is a way of thinking and doing exercised in situations of emergency or crisis, in which solutions are neither logical nor obvious. Persons of *metis* show their mettle through "a complex but very coherent body of mental attitudes and intellectual behavior which combines flair, wisdom, forethought, subtlety of mind, deception, resourcefulness, vigilance, opportunism," according to Marcel Detienne and Jean-Pierre Vernant in *Cunning Intelligence in Greek Culture and Society.*

These qualities perfectly describe a kind of popular figure found in the folklore and mythology of nearly every society, a person given to both high-minded heroics and lowdown appetites, someone as commonly called a liar, lecher, and outlaw as a role model, leader, and savior, a character sometimes depicted as a deity and sometimes as a degenerate, an individual who, like Odysseus himself, excels at living by his or her wits—the Trickster.

Trickster figures take many forms. In Europe, Till Eulenspiegel, Pippi Longstocking, Puss in Boots, and Mary Poppins are Tricksters, mischievous individuals who get out of difficult predicaments through clever and sometimes cruel stratagems. In North America, Br'er Rabbit and Appalachian Jack demonstrate the same knack for eluding catastrophe through quick thinking. Among Native Americans, Tricksters appear as animals—the coyote, raven, or hare; in Africa, as spiders, the Signifying Monkey, or divine messengers Legba and Eshu. The court jesters Tenali Rama and Birbal in India, the storyteller Scheherazade in Iran, and San Pedro and Jesucristo, Mexico's folkloric Abbott and Costello, are Tricksters, too.

The Coyote character of Native American folklore exemplifies the Trickster's mix of guile and virtue.

The Frog People had dammed the river so they and their kin would always have enough water. Coyote was extremely thirsty and gave the Frog People a beautiful shell, in exchange for which he was permitted to drink from their pond for as long as he wanted.

Coyote plunged his snout into the pond and took a deep, long drink. When he came up for air, the Frog People asked, "Are you finished?" Coyote shook his head and plunged his snout back in.

When he came up for air a second time, the Frog People asked, "Are you finished?" Coyote shook his head again and plunged his snout back in.

This went on and on, until the dam began to crumble and collapse, releasing life-giving water to the rest of the valley. All the while Coyote was drinking, he had been secretly digging a hole in the dam with his snout.

Like clowns, their cousins in impish wit, Coyote and other Tricksters revel in flouting traditions and breaking taboos. They deliberately do the opposite of what's expected:

they walk on their hands and stand on their heads; they turn their backs to the audience and say the reverse of what they mean; they wear their clothes inside out and eat excrement.

They are also capable of suspending the laws of physics. During the many misadventures of Mica, the Coyote figure of the Lakota tribe, his opponents regularly pummel and flatten him like a deerskin, then use him as a throw rug. But he always manages to puff himself back up and walk away to fight again another day.

Since Odysseus's adventure with the Trojan Horse, Tricksters have been found on battlefields, where their artifice often overcomes brute force. When the U.S. "ghost army" landed in Europe a few weeks after D-Day, the unit was made up of around a thousand men, mostly actors, writers, camouflage experts, decorators, and artists, including abstract expressionist Ellsworth Kelly and fashion designer Bill Blass. They specialized in visual and sonic trickery, creating illusions that gave the impression that much more threatening armored divisions were present. The ghost army mounted speakers on flatbed trucks and drove around blasting recordings of Sherman tanks on the march, dragging brush behind them to stir up dust, thus making it appear the force was much larger than it really was.

One trait all Tricksters share is their gift for emerging unvanquished—if not unscathed—from even the tightest binds. This sinuous ability to wriggle out of the gravest difficulties defines *metis* and is perhaps what Homer had in mind in the opening line of the *Odyssey*, in which he describes Odysseus as "polytropic," from *poly*, "many," and *tropos*, "turning": "Tell me, O Muse, of the man of many twists and turns, who wandered full many ways after he had sacked the sacred citadel of Troy."

It is through *metis* that the hero shows his worth. It is through *metis* that the heroine defeats her rivals. It is through *metis* that the quick-witted always find ways to survive and succeed. And it was through *metis* that Odysseus twisted and turned back home to the gorgeous town of Ithaca.

. . . . .

LEGBA HAD LONG resented Mawu for the way she took credit for all his good deeds and blamed him when things went wrong that were no fault of his own. So one day he decided to outwit Mawu.

Legba went to Mawu and warned her that someone planned to steal her prized yams that very night. Enraged, Mawu responded by threatening to kill anyone who dared to enter her garden. The townsfolk all were terrified, and no one went anywhere near Mawu's garden.

When it was dark and Mawu was fast asleep, Legba crept into her house, slipped into the room where she slept, and stole her sandals. He then climbed into her garden, took the plump yams, and feasted on them.

The next morning Mawu discovered the theft and spotted the prints of the thief's sandals in the dirt. Mawu assembled all the townsfolk and measured each person's feet. When none matched the prints in her garden, Legba suggested that Mawu measure her own feet.

Mawu scoffed at this idea, but Legba persisted, and she eventually relented. When Mawu measured her own feet, she saw, to her shame and consternation, that they exactly matched the prints of the thief.

·　·　·　·

TEN THOUSAND ENEMY soldiers were fast approaching along the Yangtze River, and the quivers of K'ung-ming's army were empty. It was only a matter of time before his opponents caught up with K'ung-ming and his retreating troops, to find them defenseless.

His commander, who had long resented K'ung-ming's fame and popularity among his men, ordered that a hundred thousand arrows be produced within three days. Knowing the task to be impossible, the commander planned to use K'ung-ming's failure as a pretext to execute him. K'ung-ming accepted the task, agreeing that his life would be forfeit should he fail.

K'ung-ming's face was like gleaming jade. He wore a turban around his head and held a fan crafted of crane plumes. A renowned Taoist scholar, he lived in seclusion in the countryside until enlisted by the emperor in the effort to save the failing Han dynasty. His men heard tales that K'ung-ming could change a row of beans into a line of soldiers with a wave of his sword and create a river where before there was just dry sand. They often reminded each other that K'ung-ming's name meant "vast wisdom."

So when the first day passed and K'ung-ming did nothing to produce the hundred thousand arrows, his men were calm, trusting their general's cunning.

When the second day passed and K'ung-ming still did nothing to produce the hundred thousand arrows, his men became alarmed, knowing the enemy would soon be upon them.

On the night of the third day, just as his men were beginning to panic, fearing their beloved general had failed them, a thick fog rolled up the Yangtze River. K'ung-ming instructed his troops to pack twenty small boats with straw bales, tie the boats together with long ropes, and float them downriver toward the opposing army.

When the unmanned boats silently arrived alongside the enemy camp, K'ung-ming ordered his men to begin pounding their war drums, just as during an attack. The enemy soldiers sprang from their tents and unleashed volley after volley into the dense mist, the arrows lodging harmlessly in the straw bales of the fleet. K'ung-ming then told his men to pull back the boats, each bristling with thousands of shafts.

That night K'ung-ming reported to his commander: "Three days ago, I studied the local weather and calculated tonight's fog. We have gained the hundred thousand arrows, which tomorrow we will return to our enemy."

·　　·　　·　　·

AFTER THEIR ALLIES suffered a defeat that imperiled their position, the townsfolk withdrew to their village to prepare for siege. On the Moroccan horizon, dust kicked up by the advancing enemy army was already visible. After years of war, the villagers had no more food or water. The crops had all been razed or eaten, and all the livestock slaughtered to feed the starving population.

The elders told the villagers that it was futile to resist, that they would surrender and throw themselves on the mercy of their foe. The terrified villagers agreed, hoping the enemy would pity them for all they had suffered.

Just then Aicha stepped forward and said, "There is a way to save ourselves and our village, if you will help me."

Aicha's words rallied the villagers, and they asked what she needed.

"A calf," she said.

The villagers' fragile hopes were dashed. All the animals had been eaten weeks ago. How would they ever find a calf? Aicha insisted they search, and eventually a calf was found hidden in the barn of an old miser.

"Now I need a sack of corn," Aicha said.

Again the villagers' hopes were dashed. Every kernel of grain had been eaten weeks ago. How would they ever find any corn? Aicha insisted they search, and eventually a sack of corn was found hidden in the kitchen of a shopkeeper.

Aicha took the corn, mixed it with some of the little water left in the village, and fed it to the calf.

"How can you feed precious corn to this calf when our

children are dying of hunger?" the villagers protested. Aicha ignored them.

After the calf had eaten, Aicha led it to the village gates and nudged the calf outside, where it began grazing on the grass between the village and the enemy troops, now taking up their battle formations. Aicha then ordered the village's other gates thrown open, telling her neighbors to sweep their stoops and go about their business as usual. Aicha herself sat on the village wall, an easy target for an enemy archer.

Seeing all this, the general halted his advance. He ordered his soldiers to seize the calf and kill it. Finding the undigested corn inside, he concluded the village was much better supplied than he had thought. Fearing an ambush, he ordered an immediate retreat, giving the villagers time to call in reinforcements.

·   ·   ·   ·

TENALI RAMA DISPLAYED an unusually shrewd and unruly intelligence from his earliest youth, always questioning his elders, his teachers, and his faith. A mendicant monk, impressed with the boy's wit, taught him a secret chant, telling him to go to the goddess Kali's temple and recite the chant three million times. "Then Kali herself will appear before you, with all her thousand terrible faces," the monk said.

The boy went to the temple and did as he was told. As he finished the three millionth chant, Kali appeared before him, with all her thousand terrible faces. Tenali Rama burst out laughing.

"Why do you laugh?" Kali demanded of the impudent boy.

"O mother," Tenali Rama replied, "when you catch cold, how do you wipe all those runny noses with just two hands?"

"Because you laughed at me," the incensed Kali decreed, "you will be a jester, destined to make your living only by laughter."

And so Tenali Rama joined the court of Krishnadevaraya, where he alternately amused and infuriated the monarch. Eventually, Krishnadevaraya tired of Tenali Rama's relentless impertinence, sentencing him to be buried up to his neck in the ground and have an elephant trample his head.

Krishnadevaraya's soldiers took Tenali Rama to the countryside, buried him up to his neck, and went off to fetch an elephant. Just then a hunchback wandered by and asked Tenali Rama what he was doing in the ground.

"I, too, am a hunchback," Tenali Rama lied, "and a holy man brought me to this sacred spot and buried me, saying if I remained here for one day with my eyes and my mouth firmly shut, I would be cured. Your arrival is propitious, for one day has passed. Please dig me up, and let's see if it worked."

The hunchback hurriedly complied and, after freeing Tenali Rama, saw he had no hunch.

"Please bury me so that I, too, may be cured," the hunchback pleaded. Tenali Rama hurriedly complied, reminding the man to keep his eyes and mouth firmly shut. Just then the soldiers returned with the elephant, and it trampled the hunchback's head.

When Tenali Rama returned to court, Krishnadevaraya was secretly delighted to have his jester back. He could not, however, allow disobedience to go unpunished. He once again condemned Tenali Rama to death, this time allowing him to choose his own method of execution.

Tenali Rama's choice: "Old age."

.   .   .   .

As they traveled from town to town, San Pedro and Jesucristo were often hungry. One day, San Pedro found some figs in a bag and, to keep the luscious fruit for himself, decided not to tell Jesucristo of his discovery.

When Jesucristo happened to see San Pedro sneak a fig from the bag, he asked, "What are you eating, San Pedro?"

"Just little pellets of burro dung," San Pedro replied.

Later that day, San Pedro secretly reached into the bag and popped another fig into his mouth but immediately spat it out. All the figs had become pellets of burro dung.

As San Pedro and Jesucristo traveled, the Devil shadowed them, seeking to provoke them into confrontations. One day as they rested under a cottonwood tree, the Devil appeared, saying that if San Pedro could put his fist through the trunk the Devil would admit San Pedro was stronger.

"Very well," San Pedro said. "Meet me here again tomorrow."

The next day San Pedro and Jesucristo arrived early at the cottonwood tree. Jesucristo cut a hole through the trunk and then covered it up with bark. When the Devil arrived, Jesucristo volunteered to officiate, tapping the trunk of the tree to show the combatants where to strike.

"You go first," Jesucristo said to the Devil, tapping on a solid place.

The Devil struck the tree, and his fist went into the trunk a few inches.

"Now it's your turn," Jesucristo said to San Pedro, tapping on the concealed hole.

San Pedro struck the tree where Jesucristo had indicated, and his arm went all the way through the trunk.

Enraged, the Devil challenged San Pedro to another contest—to see who could throw a stone farthest into the ocean.

"Very well," San Pedro said. "Meet me here again tomorrow."

The next day San Pedro and Jesucristo arrived at the beach to find the Devil waiting for them. Jesucristo once again volunteered to officiate. "You will throw together, on the count of three," he said.

The Devil reached down to pick up a stone, and as he did so San Pedro slipped his hand into his pocket.

"One. Two. Three!" Jesucristo said, and together the Devil and San Pedro threw. The Devil's stone soared far out to sea, eventually dropping with a splash. But San Pedro's just kept going and going, finally disappearing over the horizon. It was a small gray sparrow.

. . . . .

KING AKBAR RECEIVED a handsome, eloquent parrot as a gift, which he grew to love very much. When Akbar had to make an arduous journey, he placed the royal parrot in his servants' care. "Whoever tells me this parrot has died," Akbar warned, "will himself be put to death."

One day, despite their anxious ministrations, the servants found the parrot dead. Horrified, they turned to Birbal to break the news to Akbar upon his return.

Birbal went immediately to Akbar, urging him to come see the parrot. "He is a veritable yogi!" Birbal enthused. "He has achieved samadhi, complete one-pointedness of mind!"

Thrilled, Akbar rushed to see the parrot, only to find it stiff and lifeless on the floor.

"This parrot hasn't reached samadhi," Akbar said. "It's hopped the twig, popped its clogs, agitated the gravel and finally fallen off its perch. It's crossed the Jordan and assumed room temperature, bought the farm and been planted in the skull orchard, run down the curtain and joined the bleedin' choir invisible. This is an ex-parrot!"

"Now, you must become an ex-king," Birbal said, "for by your own decree whoever tells you this parrot has died will himself be put to death."

SLAPSTICK METAPHYSICS

*Being a rumination on the philosophical aspects of wit,
told through the structure of classic jokes*

So an Irishman walks into a bar, right, and orders three pints of Guinness. He sits at a table in the corner and takes a swig of each beer in turn, consecutive like, until he finishes them. Then he comes back, orders three more, and drinks them the same way.

The guy is new in town, so people notice but don't say anything. Eventually he becomes a regular, and the bartender finally asks why he always drinks like that.

"I've got two brothers," he says, "one in America and one in Australia, and when we left home we promised each other we'd drink this way to remember the days when we all drank together."

So one day the guy comes in and orders just two pints. The whole bar goes quiet. When he comes back for a second round, the bartender offers his condolences.

The guy thinks for a sec, then laughs and says, "No, my brothers are fine, it's just that I've quit drinking."

Ha-ha. Like that one? I got a million of 'em.

The thing about jokes, though, is, if you think about it, they're all the same. I mean, the material, the setup, the punch line—you've heard it all before, right?

Heard the one about the German, the Italian, the Mexican, and the Jew who get lost in the desert?

So the German says, "I'm tired and thirsty, I must have beer."

The Italian says, "I'm tired and thirsty, I must have wine."

The Mexican says, "I'm tired and thirsty, I must have tequila."

The Jew says, "I'm tired and thirsty, I must have diabetes."

That's basically the same joke as the one about the Irish guy and his brothers, isn't it? I mean, you set up the pattern, create the expectation like, then slip in the surprise at the last minute.

We really get a kick out of that—not getting what we expect, having the rug pulled out from under us, so to speak. Never tire of it, even though we've heard it all before.

I read this short story once, by Isaac Asimov, who wrote all those science fiction books, about this scientist, Noel Meyerhof, who wants to find out where jokes come from. Ever notice that everyone can tell a joke, Meyerhof thinks, but no one can really claim to have ever made one up? Even professional stand-ups pretty much retell the same old jokes, with a few new twists and turns.

Like that one-liner, "Take my wife . . . please." That's a story we've all heard before. And we all know how it ends. But still we laugh.

It's like, at all times and in all places, somewhere some husband is always complaining about his wife, somewhere some wife is always complaining about her husband, somewhere some Irishman is always walking into a bar.

Plus, another thing Meyerhof notices is, jokes mostly involve bad things happening to people, tragic stuff.

Heard the one about the guy with an extra Super Bowl ticket?

So this guy's making his way to his seat, right, and notices that the seat next to him is empty. He asks the guy in the next seat over if anyone will be sitting there, and the guy says no, no one will be sitting there.

"Geez, who would have a ticket to the Super Bowl and not use it?"

"The seat belongs to my wife," the guy explains. "I was supposed to come with her, but she died. This is the first Super Bowl we haven't attended together since we got married fifty years ago."

"Oh, I'm very sorry to hear that. Couldn't a family member or a friend have used the ticket, though?"

"No," the guy says. "They're all at her funeral."

Or the one about the volunteer who calls up this guy to ask him to donate to charity?

So the guy gets all offended and says, "Did you know that my mother is dying from an incurable illness? That my brother, a disabled veteran, is blind and confined to a wheelchair? That my sister's husband was killed in a car accident, leaving her penniless with three small children? Well, I don't give money to any of them, why should I give it to you?"

Tragic stuff, right? But still we laugh.

So Meyerhof feeds this massive joke book into this supercomputer called Multivac. Multivac analyzes all the jokes and spits out an answer: An alien civilization wrote all the jokes and placed them in our brains as some kind of psychology experiment. We make rats run mazes to find out how they think, and these aliens make up jokes to test our existential reflexes.

A joke is like a tap to the knee with one of those little rubber hammers, to see if our psychological defense mechanisms still work.

There is one type of joke, though, which Multivac finds original to humans—puns—because puns are made up on the spot by an identifiable individual.

Heard the one about the guy who wondered why the baseball kept getting bigger? Then it hit him.

Jokes are like pitching, I guess. Every pitcher throws the same ball, but one places it better than another.

Buster Keaton loved baseball. Used to organize pickup games between takes on set. Ever seen his flicks? They're silent. And short. You should. He does that same trick—setting up like he's going someplace and then arriving someplace else.

There's the one where his girlfriend is drowning and he throws her a life preserver, which immediately sinks.

And the one where he paints a picture of a hook on a wall and then actually hangs his hat on it.

And the one where the crazy mobile home he and his new wife just built is stuck on the tracks at a railroad crossing, and you see this big-ass steam train screaming down the line toward it, and you see the newlyweds by the side of the road holding each other, bracing for the impact, and then you see the train barrel right on by, leaving the house without a scratch.

The whole time it was on an adjacent track!

Keaton and his wife can't believe their luck and are practically jumping for joy—until suddenly another train, coming from the opposite direction, plows right into Keaton's little love nest and turns it into a heap of toothpicks.

Funny how we find misfortune so funny.

Even funnier if we think, just for a minute, that we've avoided misfortune, that the light at the end of the tunnel isn't some big-ass steam train screaming down the line toward us.

Like that old gag: This guy's walking down the street, spots a banana peel on the sidewalk, steps over it, and, while turning around to admire his accomplishment, falls into an open manhole.

Nothing like a good pratfall to lift the spirits.

Clowns turn things upside down to show things right side up.

Keaton grew up on stage, you know, in vaudeville. The Three Keatons were Keaton Jr., his mom, Myra, who played sax, and his dad, Joe, who spent most of the show throwing his son around the theater, into the scenery and the orchestra pit, and sometimes into audience members' laps. That's how he got the name "Buster." Keaton knew how to take a tumble, though, so he never got hurt much.

There's one story, when Keaton was maybe like three years old.

So his parents leave him alone in the hotel in this small midwestern town where they are playing when a cyclone sweeps through. The storm rips the roof off that hotel, sucks baby Buster right out of the room, and deposits him three or four blocks away, smack in the middle of Main Street. Like I said, Keaton knew how to take a tumble, so he wasn't hurt much. Years later he ended up putting a scene like that into one of his movies.

No matter what crazy shit is happening, Keaton never laughs. Never even cracks a smile. That's why they called him the Great Stone Face. You always see him thinking behind his eyes, though, taking everything in like, unfazed and graceful, somehow always expecting to be tripped up.

Fred Karno, the guy who made the custard pie fight so popular, used to dip his fountain pen in an empty inkwell and flick nonexistent ink into the faces of performers he was auditioning. Whoever wiped away the ink got the job.

That's what it means to be "in on" the joke, isn't it? We know that whatever can go wrong will go wrong, but it won't go wrong in any way we can predict. You've just got to go along with it.

What did Voltaire, that French philosopher, say? "God is a comedian playing to an audience that is too afraid to laugh." Even God needs a straight man, right?

Heard the one about the mountain climber who falls off a cliff?

So he grabs a tree root that's sticking out from the cliff face, and he's dangling in midair, hanging on for dear life. "Is there anybody out there?" he cries.

First there's just silence, but then he hears a voice, a deep, booming voice, that seems to come from the clouds, say, "Yes, my son, I am here. Let go of the tree root and a choir of angels will bear thee up."

The guy hesitates like, thinks for a sec, then cries: "Um, is there anybody else out there?"

Or the one about the fox that found a hole in the henhouse fence just a little too narrow to squeeze through?

So this fox is famished and weak but he fasts for three days to get thin enough to squeeze through that little hole. Once inside it's like an all-you-can-eat chicken buffet. The fox eats his fill but when he tries to squeeze back out through that little hole he's too full to fit. So he fasts for another three days until he's famished, weak, and thin enough to squeeze back out.

We go out the same way we came in, right?

So it's 1929 and the Marx Brothers are performing in Pittsburgh when the stock market crashes. The brothers' first film had just come out, they're touring with a new show, they're big stars now, and they're super-rich. But the crash wipes them out. Harpo desperately needs $10,000 to stay afloat. So he goes to see this guy he's never met, Milt Jaffe, who runs a gambling boat on the Ohio River. All he brings with him is some burnt cork.

Jaffe knows why Harpo's come, and he's all sizing him up like. But Harpo doesn't ask for any money. Instead, he starts playing a game called Pinchie Winchie. A bunch of people sit in a circle, and the first person pinches the person next to him on the nose or the cheek or the ear and that person has to pinch the next person in the same spot, and you go around and around the group as fast as you can until someone pinches in the wrong spot and drops out.

So they start playing Pinchie Winchie, and Jaffe just loves it. After each round, they bring in a new player who hasn't seen the previous game and sit that player next to Harpo. And Jaffe's nearly falling off his chair laughing. Because Harpo is rubbing his fingers on the burnt cork under the table, so every time he pinches the person next to him he leaves a big black smudge on that person's face, which everybody but that person himself can see.

Anyway, by the end of the night, Jaffe hands Harpo $10,000 in cash—no security, no interest, no signed agreement. Within a year, Harpo had earned enough to pay him back.

So it's thirty years later, and Harpo is an old man now. Not performing anymore. Several serious heart attacks. Only a couple of years left to live. He's in this bar in Vegas watching the fights on TV when he spots none other than Milt Jaffe. They get to talking, catching up on the news like, and Harpo is kind of idly playing with a pack of matches, lighting them one by one, blowing them out, and dropping them in an ashtray. Finally, he asks Jaffe why he gave him that loan all those years ago.

Jaffe thinks a bit and says, "You knew how to have a good time without spending any money."

Harpo looks at him and says, "You wouldn't lend me two bits now, would you?"

Jaffe doesn't answer, gets up to go, puts out his hand to say goodbye, but Harpo gives his cheek a quick squeeze instead— "Pinchie Winchie!"

Jaffe laughs and walks away through the bar—with a big black smudge right on his kisser because Harpo had been rubbing his fingers on the heads of the burnt matches the whole time they had been talking.

Wit is just throwing a pie in the universe's face, isn't it?

You know the French word *spirituel* means "witty" like in a joke as well as "spiritual" like in a religion? It's true. I always thought that made a lot of sense, having the funniest and the most serious stuff packed into the same word like that.

Heard the one about the Muslim guru Mullah Nasruddin?

So, over the years, the mullah acquired a lot of disciples, who followed him everywhere he went. Whatever he did, they did, too.

One day he's walking through the bazaar, and they are all tagging along behind him like. When he stops and throws his hands in the air, they stop and throw their hands in the air, too.

When he stops, touches his toes, and then leaps in the air shouting, "Moo!" they stop, touch their toes, and then leap in the air shouting, "Moo!" too.

While all this is going on, the mullah bumps into an old friend he hasn't seen for ages. "Nasruddin, who are these jokers and why are they following you?"

"I've become a sheikh," says the mullah, "and I'm instructing my disciples in achieving enlightenment."

"And how do you know when they've achieved enlightenment?"

"Easy. Every time I turn around, I count the disciples still following me. The ones who have stopped following me have achieved enlightenment."

Ha-ha. Like that one? I got a million of 'em.

An ambiguity, in ordinary speech, means something
very pronounced, and as a rule witty or deceitful.

WILLIAM EMPSON

THE CHAINS OF HABIT

*In which the author demonstrates how witty
ambiguities break bad perceptual habits*

O N   T H E   C A M P U S of Cornell University, in the gorgeous
Upstate New York town of Ithaca, an unidentified white
male in his twenties wearing a crimson windbreaker and holding
a map stops to ask directions to Olin Library of a balding, gray-
haired white male with glasses wearing a green blazer.

The balding, gray-haired white male with glasses wearing the
green blazer is giving directions to Olin Library to the unidentified white male in his twenties wearing the crimson windbreaker
and holding the map when two other unidentified white males
in their twenties pass between them carrying a door. The passing
door briefly occludes the faces of the unidentified white males in
their twenties from the balding, gray-haired white male's line of
sight.

Blocked from view behind the passing door, the unidentified white male in his twenties wearing the crimson windbreaker
and holding the map changes places with one of the unidentified
white males in their twenties carrying the door, the one wearing
a green windbreaker and holding a map.

The unidentified white male in his twenties wearing the crimson windbreaker and holding the map walks off with the door,
while the balding, gray-haired white male with glasses wearing

the green blazer continues giving directions to Olin Library to the unidentified white male in his twenties wearing the green windbreaker and holding the map, the one who until recently was carrying the door.

The balding, gray-haired white male with glasses wearing the green blazer stands next to the unidentified white male in his twenties wearing the green windbreaker, who until recently was carrying the door, takes the map from his hands, and shows him the route to Olin Library—unaware that he is talking to an entirely different person from the one who originally requested his help.

This experiment, performed in the late 1990s, is a demonstration of change blindness, in which significant alterations in a subject's field of vision go completely unnoticed. Change blindness typically occurs when a disturbance or interruption distracts a viewer from the object of attention. Show subjects a flickering picture of a barn next to a pond, and it takes some time to notice that the barn's reflection in the water shifts position from one flicker to the next. Without the flicker, the change is easily seen.

The door study was among the first to show change blindness in the real world. On average, only between a third and one-half of subjects notice something is amiss in these experiments.

Change blindness suggests that we often don't pay very close attention to the world. Attention is effort, so it makes cognitive sense that the brain would not retain every detail of every situation but only those that seem germane or crucial in the moment. The brain estimates the importance of visual information before storing it, and if something seems noteworthy or different, we heed it. What inures is ignored.

Much of what we think of as observation is actually assumption. We don't so much see as surmise what's in front of us. We perceive what we suspect is there. "It is the expected that happens," as psychologist Joseph Jastrow put it in "The Mind's Eye," his 1899 essay about the influence of mental states on seeing.

Perception is a habit, and habit is the enemy of wit.

Transport for London, the local government agency responsible for the British capital's public transportation system, showcased how pervasive this inattention is in a 2008 advertisement promoting cycle awareness.

The scene: an elegant parlor in Lord Smithe's stately home. Oil paintings, tapestries, and hunting trophies adorn the walls. A lavish fern stands beside the window curtains, and a vase of red carnations sits on a side table. A rumpled Columbo-esque detective wearing a dark raincoat and holding a fedora interrogates the suspects: the maid, who holds a bed warmer and stands in front of a rearing stuffed black bear; the white-gloved butler holding a rolling pin; and Lady Smithe, who wears a sun hat and holds a flowerpot. All the while a stiff-backed police constable jots down notes in a notebook.

Lord Smithe himself lies on the carpet, quite dead due to the impact on his skull of a blunt instrument. A brown mantelpiece clock lies toppled over by his head.

As the detective begins his questioning, the camera zooms in on his face and then pans across to close-ups of the faces of each suspect as they provide their alibis: the maid was "polishing the brass" in the master bedroom; the butler was "buttering His Lordship's scones belowstairs"; Lady Smithe, so recently widowed, was planting petunias in the potting shed.

The detective briskly instructs the constable to arrest—spoiler alert!—Lady Smithe, since as any horticulturalist knows you don't plant petunias until May is out.

The mystery, however, is just beginning.

.　.　.　.

EVERYTHING HAS HABITS. The crow's-feet that come from squinting or laughter, the crease in a treasured and oft-opened letter, the ruts worn in a path frequently traveled—-all are creatures of habit, created by repeatedly performing the same action.

Even neurons have habits. When continuously exposed to a fixed stimulus, neurons become steadily less sensitive to that stimulus—until they eventually stop responding to it altogether.

Whereas change blindness masks a difference that might otherwise be obvious, another form of unseeing, persistence blindness, hides the obvious in plain sight. Anything that's habitually encountered—the landscape of a daily commute, shopfronts passed on a walk to the bus stop, photographs arranged on a mantelpiece—tends toward invisibility.

The more we see a thing, the less we see it. Familiarity breeds neglect. Significant others become usual suspects.

"We see the object as though it were enveloped in a sack," lamented Victor Shklovsky, part of the Russian formalist group, a loose affiliation of early twentieth century literary and artistic theorists. "Habituation devours objects, clothes, furniture, one's wife, and the fear of war. If all the complex lives of many people go on unconsciously, then such lives are as if they have never been."

Shklovsky offered *ostranenie*, or "defamiliarization," as an alternative to habitual ways of seeing that render much of the world invisible. For Shklovsky, the purpose of art was to defamiliarize: to estrange us from routine perceptions, to make the commonplace uncommon again. "Art removes objects from the automatism of perception," Shklovsky argued. "Art exists that one may recover the sensation of life; it exists to make one feel things, to make the stone *stony.*"

Art recovers the sensation of life, Shklovsky believed, through ambiguity, the quandary caused when, as in puns, meanings are multiplied, when at least two understandings—one orthodox and authorized, the other perhaps seditious or obscene—are equally present and plausible. Ambiguity forces us to view the familiar with fresh eyes, if only to decide which of all possible meanings might actually apply.

Around the same time that Shklovsky was praising ambiguity, Soviet censors sought to systematically impose *odnoznachnost*, or "one-meaningness," on all forms of public communication. The erection of a statue of Sergei Kirov in Petrozavodsk offers a case study in the subversive use of witty ambiguity.

In the autumn of 1936, the good citizens of Petrozavodsk, the capital of the Russian region of Karelia, which runs along the border with Finland, unveiled a monument to swashbuckling Bolshevik Sergei Kirov. Kirov had been assassinated two years earlier, a murder that helped precipitate the Great Purge, the wave of repression, surveillance, and executions meant to cleanse the Communist Party of Joseph Stalin's foes. The Great Purge was accompanied by a meticulous campaign of censorship in which Soviet apparatchiks attempted to eliminate every possible interpretation of words and pictures except those officially sanctioned by the regime.

Censors took extreme measures to prevent double meanings from reaching the public, including by inspecting individual newspaper pages to detect potentially subversive wordplay or image juxtaposition. Using this method on a 1937 issue of the Moscow broadsheet *Trud*, one diligent censor discovered that when held to the light a certain photograph of a worker wielding a hammer on one side of the page seemed to be striking the head of a portrait of Stalin on the other.

Soon after the Kirov monument was finished, a local Petrozavodsk party chief complained that the Communist leader's pose—left hand in pocket; index finger of the right hand extended in a slight curl, pointing down and forward—was uncharacteristic of the man himself. In addition, he had his back to Karl Marx Avenue, an affront to party ideology. Worst of all, when seen from the entrance to the city's summer garden, Kirov's right hand bore a suspicious resemblance to male genitalia.

Sergei Kirov's ambiguous finger, as seen from the entrance
to the city of Petrozavodsk's summer garden

The statue's ambiguous finger forced viewers to ask: Is Kirov striking a pensive pose, or is this a penis which I see before me?

The brain, despite perceptual hiccups like change blindness

and persistence blindness, strives to make the world predictable, just like Soviet censors tried to do through the imposition of "one-meaningness." But once perception settles into a comfortable pattern, we fall asleep to it—and it is only when the pattern is broken that we notice that there is a pattern at all.

The chains of habit are too weak to be felt until they are too strong to be broken, to paraphrase Samuel Johnson.

Verbal and visual wit kick bad perceptual habits by exploiting ambiguity, the gap between what we expect and what we encounter, what we see and what we get. By adopting a skewed perspective, ironists, satirists, and dissidents can get away with saying one thing because no one can be really sure that they are not saying something else.

. . . . .

ONE-MEANINGNESS IS ALIVE and well in China, where the government is prosecuting a censorship campaign every bit as meticulous as that of the Soviets in the 1930s and where unauthorized ambiguity can still get you into a lot of trouble, as it did one day for an editor at the liberal paper *Southern Metropolis News*.

On the day in question, the front page of *Southern Metropolis News* featured a quote from a speech by President Xi Jinping as the headline at the top of the page. It read, from left to right: "The media run by the party and the government are a base for propaganda and must display complete loyalty to the party."

Directly beneath that headline was a photograph of friends and relations of Yuan Geng, a prominent reformist who had recently died, scattering his ashes at sea. In the top right corner of that photograph was another headline, which read, from left to right: "The soul returns to the sea."

If, however, the last two characters on each line of the Xi Jinping headline are read from top to bottom, rather than from left to right, in conjunction with the Yuan Geng headline in the photo directly below them, the text reads: "Media displaying complete loyalty to the party have their souls returned to the sea."

Did *Southern Metropolis News* intend its front page to make such a dark statement about the predicament of the free press? The ambiguity was enough to get an editor fired for the headline.

Though the Chinese government rigorously roots out ambiguity in public discourse, it does not apply that same prohibition to itself. Official Communist Party communications are typically couched in what's known as "fruit language." Words like "apple" and "banana" are specific and precise, but the word "fruit" is generic and imprecise, open to a range of possible meanings. The bureaucratic virtue of fruit language is its ambiguity, allowing the speaker to keep his motivations and preferences obscure while leaving his subordinates to divine the appropriate interpretation.

Before the crackdown in Tiananmen Square on June 4, 1989, Chinese Premier Li Peng backed the use of force against the demonstrators, while his predecessor Zhao Ziyang opposed it. Asked his opinion, State Council secretariat Luo Gan replied, in fluent fruit: "I am certain justice will prevail." If the crackdown was a success, Zhao Ziyang could say he had sided with Li Peng all along; if the crackdown failed, he could say he had always opposed it.

Ambiguity gives dissidents leeway for free speech even as it creates wiggle room through which double-talking politicians can escape.

In Roman mythology, Janus was the god of beginnings and endings, of physical as well as spiritual transitions, and, therefore, of doorways, portals, and passages of all kinds. He was depicted as two-faced, with the faces each looking in opposite directions, to symbolize his multiple perspectives, his simultaneous views of past and future, his dual outlook on veracity and deceit.

In the 1970s, psychiatrist Albert Rothenberg coined the term "Janusian thinking" to describe the early, inspirational stage of the creative process, during which, he argued, an individual simultaneously holds antithetical ideas in mind. Rather than try to reconcile these ideas, Rothenberg theorized that Janusians discard previously accepted scientific, theoretical, and artistic canons and use the friction created by opposing ideas to generate new hypotheses.

For Rothenberg, Danish physicist Niels Bohr was a model of Janusian thinking. Bohr was the first to articulate the principle of complementarity, a fundamental tenet of quantum mechanics, which states that subatomic particles like photons exist simultaneously both as waves and particles. It is impossible to observe or measure the wave and particle states at the same time, because whether a photon behaves like a wave or a particle depends on the experimental conditions—and, crucially, on the disposition of the observer.

Before Bohr, classical theory held that the behavior of physical bodies and forces could be precisely known. The principle of complementarity showed that at the subatomic level those rules did not apply. Sometimes particles had one set of behaviors and characteristics, sometimes another, depending on the circumstances. There was "no question of a choice between two different concepts," according to Bohr, "but rather the description of two complementary sides of the same phenomenon."

You can't get into the habit of perceiving a photon as either a wave or a particle because it is always both things at once.

Each electron is a Janus, always having two opposing faces, but turning only one of them toward us at any given moment. At the subatomic level, reality itself is ambiguous. Things both are and are not what they seem. The universe is witty, made up of quantum puns—particles with the ability to hold themselves in two different states at the same time.

. . . . .

THE COMPLEMENTARITY PRINCIPLE is hard for us to fathom because, in the physical world, we find it difficult to pay attention to more than one thing at a time, much less to grasp how one thing can exist simultaneously in two different states. This is evident from multiple-object tracking (MOT) experiments.

In a MOT test, participants see eight identical dots on a screen. Before the experiment begins, four dots flash to mark their status as targets. Then all the dots move randomly around the screen. The task: identify the original targets when all the dots stop.

Most people can't keep track of more than one or two dots at once.

While multiple-object tracking may be challenging, tracking multiple meanings is easy. Indeed, this is how wit and ambiguity work together.

We have an innate ability to hold in our minds multiple meanings about the same thing at the same time. Which meaning ultimately emerges as primary depends on the experimental conditions—and, crucially, on the disposition of the observer.

There is even evidence that, when it comes to the visual arts, we prefer work that presents ambiguous interpretive challenges over work that is more straightforward and easier to interpret.

In one study, researchers showed participants photographs of ambiguous works of art—including pieces by Hans Bellmer, a

German artist known for his macabre life-sized female dolls, and Magritte's *Les Jours Gigantesques*, a painting in which a female nude is being assaulted, or possibly embraced, by a male figure wearing a brown jacket. Viewers rated each work according to its intellectual and emotional impact and how much they said they liked it.

The research team then showed participants photographs of the works again, this time asking them to rate each work according to its level of ambiguity and how easily they felt its meaning could be resolved. They found that the higher an artwork's subjectively perceived ambiguity, the more participants said they liked it and the more they experienced it as both intellectually interesting and emotionally affecting.

It was the ambiguity itself that viewers found aesthetically pleasing, the researchers concluded. The more a work invited and, in some ways, resisted inquiry, the more compelling viewers tended to regard it. The process of working through the ambiguities, not the arrival at any conclusive interpretation, was what stimulated intellectual interest and emotion. This study followed earlier research by the same team that found viewers preferred simple two-tone images when they felt they could detect hidden figures within the work, again suggesting that the allure of ambiguity accounted for the pieces' appeal.

The mind enjoys disporting itself among ambiguities.

In the Transport for London ad, as the police constable escorts Lady Smithe to the station, the detective turns to the camera and asks, "How observant were you?" in noticing the changes introduced into the proceedings. At which point the screen fades to black, and when the video resumes we see a wide-angle shot of the full set, complete with lights, cameras, actors, and technicians. The teleplay unfolds again, but this time we are eyewitnesses to how the scene of the crime is altered. (If you want to test your powers of observation, search online for "Transport for London Whodunnit.")

As the main camera zooms in for close-ups of the faces of the detective and suspects, stagehands rush in and replace the armchair in the corner with a settee; lilies arrive in place of the carnations; the butler trades his rolling pin for a candlestick and Lady Smithe her flowerpot for a cactus (she also exchanges her sun hat for a cloche); the stuffed black bear exits in favor of a knight in armor; the oil paintings, tapestries, and hunting trophies are displaced by garish military portraits; the detective gets a light-colored raincoat instead of a dark one (as well as a new hat); a Greek bust, possibly of Aristotle, appears where the fern had been; even the corpse, now lying on a different carpet, is other, the original balding man in a navy blue blazer having crawled away as a gray-haired man with glasses in a green blazer crawled in.

In all, twenty-one changes are made to the scene between the establishing shot of the parlor and the dramatic denouement of Lady Smithe's indictment. The first time I watched the video, I spotted just one: the brown mantelpiece clock is swapped for a faux-marble-columned one.

The point of this Transport for London public service announcement was to impress upon drivers how easy it is to overlook cyclists on the road. It also impresses upon us how habitual perceptions can blind us to major changes taking place right in front of us—and how the witty acuity of vision prompted by ambiguity opens our eyes to a multiplicity of meanings.

To see clearly, look askance.

> What a lucky find reveals first is neither
> cosmos nor chaos but the mind of the finder.
>
> LEWIS HYDE

finding minds

*Being an account of the relationship between wit
and discovery, modeled on the 1754 letter by English
author Horace Walpole to his friend Horace Mann
in which he invented the word "serendipity"*

Dear Horace,

*Your description of the Transport for London advertisement
reminds me of Heller's observation that the structure of the pun is,
in several crucial respects, identical to that of other, more respectable
literary genres, especially the detective story. In a detective story, the
sleuth solves the crime by deducing facts from scattered scraps of
information and by connecting seemingly unrelated observations.
Just so when deciphering puns: the listener "solves" a pun by bringing
together previously hidden or unsuspected associations.*

 *In thinking about the Transport for London ad, though, it
occurred to me that forms of wit other than the pun can also be
understood as compressed detective stories. I'm thinking in particular
of people who "live by their wits," as the saying goes: inventors,
scientists, and innovators of all kinds, people skilled in improvising
fixes, finding clever escapes from tight scrapes, or making unlikely
discoveries under seemingly inauspicious conditions.*

Take Alfredo Moser, for example. When he started tinkering with plastic bottles filled with water, he was looking for an alternative to matches. Like many cities in the developing world, Uberaba, Moser's hometown in southern Brazil, has unreliable supplies of almost everything, including electricity. Residents depend on candles or kerosene lamps during the frequent blackouts. But in trying to craft a cheap lens that could focus the sun's rays with sufficient strength to start a fire, Moser made a different discovery: empty plastic bottles can also serve nicely as light bulbs.

Moser filled a bottle with water, added a capful of bleach to prevent algae growth, cut a hole in his roof, snugly fit the bottle halfway into it and sealed the edges. During the day, the water in the bottle refracted sunlight, providing illumination equivalent to a forty-watt bulb—at no cost. Moser started installing his "liters of light" in his neighbors' dark, makeshift shacks, allowing them to work, read, or study indoors. Moser lamps are now in place in countries ranging from Tanzania to Bangladesh.

Discoveries like this are usually chalked up to serendipity, the accidental solution to a problem the problem-solver isn't consciously trying to solve. But I would argue that serendipity is actually a sophisticated form of wit, one that leaves little or nothing to chance, relying instead on rather acute powers of attention and observation.

The story of the word "serendipity" itself demonstrates my point, so, as I have nothing better to tell you, let me recount the tale of the Three Princes of Serendip, from which I derived the term.

In ancient times there lived in the country of Serendip a wise and powerful king by the name of Giaffer. King Giaffer had three sons who were very dear to him, and, being a good father as well as a benevolent monarch, he entrusted their education only to the most excellent scholars.

As the princes grew in knowledge, wisdom, and virtue, King

Giaffer desired to test them. So he summoned each in turn, declaring that he intended to relinquish his crown to them so he could retire to a life of seclusion and contemplation. Each prince in turn declined, affirming that their father should rule until his death.

King Giaffer was well pleased with his sons, but still desired to test them further. So, feigning anger for defying his wishes, he sent the princes from Serendip to make their way as strangers in strange lands.

One day, as the princes wandered across a foreign desert kingdom, they encountered a merchant who had lost a camel. When the merchant asked if they had seen it, they replied truthfully that they had not. But they asked the merchant if the camel happened to be blind in one eye, missing a tooth, lame in one leg, and bearing a cargo of honey on one side and butter on the other.

The merchant, astounded at the accuracy of this description, confirmed that all of this was so and asked again if the princes had seen the camel. When they replied, again truthfully, that they had not, he accused them of stealing the animal and took them to Emperor Beramo for punishment.

Emperor Beramo asked the princes how they could provide such an accurate description of the camel if they had never seen it.

The princes knew the camel was blind in one eye, they explained, because they observed that grass had been eaten from one side of the road only, the side that was far less verdant, so they inferred the camel was blind on that side, otherwise it would have eaten of the lusher grass.

The princes knew the camel had lost a tooth because clumps of chewed grass about the size of a camel's tooth lay strewn along the side of the road, so they deduced that the clumps fell out of the animal's mouth through the gap left by a missing tooth.

The princes knew the camel was lame in one leg because the animal's tracks showed only three clear hoofprints, the fourth being dragged.

The princes knew the camel was bearing a cargo of honey on one side and butter on the other side because ants, which love fat, had been attracted to the melted butter on one side of the road and flies, which love sugar, had been attracted to the spilled honey on the other side.

Just as the princes finished their explanation, a traveler arrived leading a camel he had found wandering in the desert that exactly matched this description. Emperor Beramo lavished a rich reward on the princes and appointed them his advisers.

I've remarked before that serendipity is the ability to make discoveries, by accident and sagacity, of things you are not in quest of. But I would amend that definition now to state that, while serendipitous realizations might appear accidental, they are, in fact, the result of deliberate and persistent observation. Detective stories perfectly illustrate my point.

In Edgar Allan Poe's "The Murders in the Rue Morgue," considered among the very first detective stories, the narrator befriends a certain C. Auguste Dupin, a mysterious young gentleman from an illustrious family fallen on hard times who comes to Paris to seek his fortune. When a mother and daughter are brutally murdered in a nearby apartment building—the young woman throttled to death and shoved feet-first up the chimney, and the old woman hurled into the courtyard with her throat so thoroughly cut that when the police lifted her up her head fell off—the two men decide to investigate.

Arriving at the apartment, they find it in the wildest disorder, though nothing of value has been stolen, including four thousand francs in gold found under the overturned bedstead. All the windows and doors are locked from within.

As to the solution of this horrible mystery, the Parisian police haven't the slightest clue.

Dupin meticulously examines the murder scene and, indeed, the entire neighborhood immediately surrounding the apartment building. He discovers, among other things, a piece of ribbon with a knot in it peculiar to a small group of mariners, that the marks on the daughter's throat do not match the dimensions of any human hand, and that the nail holding the sash in place was broken off at the shank so the window was not, in fact, locked from the inside after all.

From this he correctly concludes that the murder was committed by an escaped orangutan owned by a French sailor serving on a Maltese vessel.

In describing the acute attention paid to the scene by Dupin, a model for later detectives like Father Brown, Sherlock Holmes, Hercule Poirot, Columbo, and your Transport for London sleuth, Poe wrote that "the difference in the extent of the information obtained lies not so much in the validity of the inference as in the quality of the observation."

Wit also relies on the quality of observation. In serendipitous endeavors, what is eventually found may not always be what was initially sought, but it is always the wit's observational power that leads to discoveries. And if I may trouble you with another tale, I think the story of how insulin was discovered will help clarify my point.

In 1921, Canadian physician Frederick Banting and medical student Charles H. Best, working with pancreatic extracts from dogs, identified insulin as the hormone that metabolizes glucose from carbohydrates. Before this discovery, individuals with type 1 diabetes faced a slow, wasting death because their pancreases had ceased to produce insulin, making it impossible for their bodies to release and use the energy stored in glucose.

However, the first clues about the role of insulin had been observed some thirty years before, in the late 1880s, when German physicians Joseph von Mering and Oskar Minkowski began removing the pancreases from dogs to study that organ's role in the digestive process.

One day, a lab assistant called attention to a swarm of flies feeding on a puddle of urine from a dog that recently had its pancreas removed. Curious, Von Mering and Minkowski tested the urine and found it soaked with glucose; in diabetes, the body tries to rid itself through urination of all the glucose it can't use.

The researchers realized that they had inadvertently created a diabetic condition in the dog by removing its pancreas, theorizing for the first time that the pancreas must secrete a hormone that metabolizes glucose. It was Banting, Best, and colleagues who later identified that hormone as insulin and developed regular insulin injections as an effective treatment for managing diabetes.

As Louis Pasteur noted, "In the fields of observation, chance favors only the prepared mind." And the prepared mind, my friend, is the witty mind.

Indulge me with one more example from the sciences.

As a boy growing up in The Hague in the 1910s, Dutch biologist Nikolaas Tinbergen was fascinated by the fish and fowl inhabiting the little pond in his backyard. These early encounters with the wildlife of the Netherlands informed his later work, and as an adult he kept an aquarium in his home.

One day he noticed that the male three-spined sticklebacks (which have "gorgeous nuptial colors," Tinbergen observed, "red on the throat and breast, greenish-blue on the back") in the tank by the window went into attack mode—head down and dorsal fin up, a posture normally assumed only in the presence of a rival male—every time a red postal van parked outside.

*Wondering whether the fish were reacting to the postal van,
Tinbergen introduced variously colored objects into the tank. He
discovered that the males became aggressive in response to anything
red—the unmistakable sign of another male's presence—regardless of
whether it actually resembled a three-spined stickleback. The
observation sparked Tinbergen's discovery of color's influence on
animal behavior, for which he shared the Nobel Prize for Physiology
or Medicine in 1973.*

*Serendipitous wits are first-class noticers who—like the three
princes who noticed the flies around the spilled honey, the lab assistant who noticed the flies around the dog's urine, and Tinbergen who
noticed the stickleback response to anything red—pay keen attention
to their environment, make strategic observations about anomalous
or unusual aspects of the objects and people around them, and translate those observations into actionable insights or useful inventions.*

*These kinds of do-it-yourself wits are what French anthropologist
Claude Lévi-Strauss called* bricoleurs, *individuals skilled in making
things from odds and ends, scraps and rejects, and whatever else they
happen to find at hand.*

Lévi-Strauss used bricoleur *to describe how cultures assemble
myths from bits and pieces of ancient stories, but the term applies
equally well to people like Alfredo Moser, whose wits, quickened into
serendipity, enable them to build something beneficial from
bric-a-brac.*

*Now, you might wonder whether this type of wit is innate—you
either have it or you don't—or whether it might not be in some form
nurtured and cultivated. Well, it turns out there is a way to hone the
powers of attention and observation needed for serendipitous discovery: live in a foreign country.*

*When you live abroad, everything is different—from the couture
to the customs, the food to the faucets. In China, leaving food on your*

*plate is a sign of appreciation that your host provided enough to eat;
in the United States, the same gesture is an insult, suggesting you
didn't enjoy your meal.*

*As you know, I was an expat for twenty-three years, happily
acclimating myself to such unfamiliar experiences as driving on the
left-hand side of the road in the United Kingdom and in the
Netherlands eating raw, salted herring with a chaser of* jenever
*(pronounced "jə'-ne-vər"), a gin made from juniper berries. My
mother once sampled this Dutch national spirit, but she didn't much
care for it. "I know why they call it that," she said, "because once you
taste it,* jenever *want to drink it again."*

*One staple of the Low Countries diet for which I never acquired
a taste was* hagelslag, *the flavored sprinkles into which natives of
other countries dip ice-cream cones but which the Dutch scatter atop
thick, dry, buttered biscuits and eat for lunch or breakfast.*

*As part of an investigation into "cognitive flexibility," the ability
to simultaneously think about multiple concepts, Dutch researchers
asked subjects to prepare* hagelslag *sandwiches in one of two ways—
the conventional way (put biscuit on plate, butter biscuit, strew
sprinkles on top) and the unconventional way (pour sprinkles on
plate, butter biscuit, press buttered side of biscuit into sprinkles).*

*After making their meals, both groups had two minutes to think
of as many uses as possible for a brick.*

*The what-can-I-do-with-a-brick quiz, otherwise known as the
Unusual Uses Test (UUT), is a creativity measure developed in 1967
by psychologist J. P. Guilford. People taking the UUT have two minutes to come up with as many applications as possible for everyday
objects, such as a paper clip, a coffee mug, or a brick. Degrees of creativity are suggested not just by how many potential uses a person can
think of, but by the number of different categories into which those
potential uses fall.*

Someone whose answers to the brick question are "paperweight," "diving aid" and "dumbbell," for example, would score lower on the UUT than someone whose answers are "projectile," "heat it up as bed warmer," and "mock coffin for a Barbie funeral." The first set of answers all fall into one category ("heavy things") while the second set of answers all fall into different categories ("weapon," "domestic appliance," "toy"), each of which is far removed from the others.

In the hagelslag experiment, those who made their sandwiches the unconventional way, by pressing the buttered biscuit into the sprinkles, scored higher on Guilford's criteria, suggesting greater facility at devising unusual uses and, therefore, greater cognitive flexibility. The researchers concluded that the break in routine afforded by the alternative method of hagelslag preparation stimulated innovative thinking.

What living abroad and the hagelslag experiment have in common is that both involve "schema violations"; that is, an experience that violates an expected sequence of events. These unusual interruptions enhance cognitive flexibility by creating cracks in habitual thinking routines just wide enough for novel ideas to squeeze through. Individuals with this kind of psychological suppleness are less prone to fixed ideas and more likely to imagine things atypically.

Serendipitous wit might therefore be defined as a knack for self-imposed schema violations, a state of mind in which one attends to the world with the freshness and specificity of someone living in a foreign country. This is the knack that enabled the three princes to so accurately describe a camel they had never seen, that permitted C. Auguste Dupin to deduce that a murderous orangutan was on the loose, and that caused Von Mering and Minkowski to postulate the existence of insulin.

When he wasn't observing three-spined sticklebacks, Tinbergen spent a lot of time with adult herring gull hens, which have pronounced orange spots on their lower mandibles. For the first few weeks of a chick's life, its mother's beak is its sole food source, and that orange spot provides a good target for chicks to aim at when engaging in the pecking behavior that prompts the mother to regurgitate food.

Tinbergen noticed that the chicks in his lab, like the male sticklebacks in his aquarium, aggressively pecked not just at their mothers' beaks, but at anything with an orange spot on it. It occurred to him that it might be possible to improve upon nature, to "make a dummy that would stimulate the chick still more than the natural object," he wrote.

So Tinbergen started making "super-gulls"—cobbled-together constructions that amplified the orange spot to which the chicks so enthusiastically responded. He painted orange spots on everything from old pieces of wood to common kitchen utensils. He made the orange spots bigger, surrounding them with white rings to enhance the contrast. No matter how exaggerated the presentation, the chicks pecked at absolutely everything—as long as it had an orange spot on it. And the bigger the spot, the more aggressively the chicks pecked.

Tinbergen called these exaggerated orange spots "supernormal stimuli," which, he concluded, "offer stimulus situations that are even more effective than the natural situation."

This response to supernormal stimuli is not limited to herring gulls. Chicks from all species will beg for food from a fake bill if it has more dramatic markings than their actual parents', and parents will ignore their own eggs and attempt to incubate much larger objects—including volleyballs—if those objects are decorated to resemble eggs.

Tinbergen concluded that human beings are susceptible to supernormal stimuli, too. The oversized eyes of stuffed animals, dolls, and cartoon characters are supernormal, he theorized, kick-starting *our instinctive response to nurture anything with infantile facial features. Sugar-saturated soft drinks, works of art, clothing, perfume, and even lipstick—anything that intensifies or exaggerates an instinctive biological or physical response—can be considered supernormal stimuli.*

"Deeply rooted in man," Tinbergen wrote, "is the same type of reactivity, and however deeply it may be covered by all types of higher mental processes, on some occasions these innate foundations of our sensory world become visible."

Supernormal stimuli, I suggest, are at work in visual wit, which opens new perspectives on the familiar by deliberately skewing or exaggerating our usual patterns of perception. We respond to these witty objects more intensely than to "normal" objects in ordinary life, just as Tinbergen's chicks responded more intensely to the exaggerated orange spots.

Often, a tweak is all that's needed to make the well-worn witty.

"Humor at its best is a kind of heightened truth—a super-truth," E. B. White wrote. I would argue this is also true of visual wit, which takes routine seeing and heightens it by shearing mundane objects of their habitual context, revealing them as suddenly strange and unfamiliar.

Visual wit is serendipitous, too. It relies on the same powers of attention and observation—and the same bricoleur-like gift for making beautiful or useful things from inauspicious stuff—that allowed Alfredo Moser to spot a light bulb in a plastic bottle filled with water.

Visual wit, like the best detective work, lies in the quality of the observation. And that is no accident.

Yours,
Horace

AMBIGUOUS FIGURES

Being an illustrated tour of visual wit,
executed in the manner of an art historical lecture

Good evening, ladies and gentlemen, and thank you for coming
out this evening.

I'd like to begin with a little quiz . . . What's this?

The Loch Ness Monster? The partially buried handle of an
ancient gardening implement? Maybe a Viking warrior submerged up to the tip of his helmet in a lake?

It's none of these things, of course. It's just three thick black
squiggles on a plain white background. What we "see" is the

brain roughly assembling possible objects from bits and pieces in its visual field.

I begin my lecture this evening with this little optical illusion because it demonstrates how seeing is an interpretive act, not merely the objective registration of external facts.

Psychologist Joseph Jastrow wrote in "The Mind's Eye," an essay published in *Popular Science* in 1899:

> True seeing, observing, is a double process, partly objective or outward—the thing seen and the retina—and partly subjective or inward—the picture mysteriously transferred to the mind's representative, the brain, and there received and affiliated with other images.
>
> —JOSEPH JASTROW

Jastrow took a special interest in optical and psychological illusions. At the University of Wisconsin–Madison, he set up a laboratory to investigate the quirks of sensory perception, including hypnosis, self-deception, and the influence of subliminal stimuli on judgment. He also took an interest in mediums and psychics, joining magician Harry Houdini onstage to debunk the claims of spiritualists.

One visual trick still bears his name.

In a Jastrow illusion, which you see here, two curved shapes of identical dimensions appear to differ in length when placed next to each other. Reverse the positions of the shapes, and you also reverse the impression of which is longer.

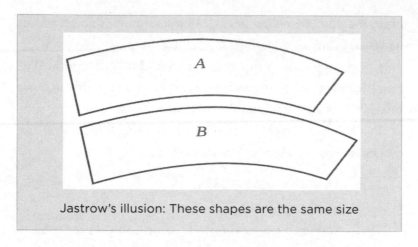

Jastrow's illusion: These shapes are the same size

Not only are our visual perceptions unreliable, Jastrow pointed out, we also tend to see things that aren't really there—human faces in rock outcroppings, battleships in cloud formations, a fish in a piece of driftwood—a phenomenon known as pareidolia, from the Greek words *para* ("beside" or "alongside of") and *eidōlon* ("image" or "shape").

Pareidolia has a long and illustrious history in art. Leonardo da Vinci, for one, recommended looking for concealed forms in ordinary objects as a technique for "opening the mind and putting it upon the scent of new thoughts," writing in his notebooks:

> If you look upon an old wall covered with dirt or the odd appearance of some streaked stones, you may discover several things like landscapes, battles, clouds, uncommon attitudes, humorous faces, draperies.
>
> —LEONARDO DA VINCI

Regular sightings of the faces of Jesus and the Virgin Mary in toast and other breakfast staples are, Jastrow argued, examples of how "the human eye detects and often creates the resemblances."

So is Brazilian artist Vik Muniz's *Medusa Marinara* (1998), a version of Caravaggio's famous *Medusa* (1590) made from leftover spaghetti and tomato sauce.

And so was my vision of a haunted visage in a serving of salted cod brandade I once ate.

In the image, which you can see here because I captured it before consuming the salted cod brandade in question, a face is clearly visible in the upper right section of the hors d'oeuvre. Heavy brows shade pinprick eyes looking anxiously downward to the viewer's right. Below them, there is a broad, almost snout-like nose above a small, tight-lipped mouth and dimpled chin. The wisps of brandade around the face suggest wild, windblown hair and a thick beard, giving the whole an appearance of some hirsute early human ancestor who has just taken fright.

The frightened face in my salted cod brandade

Images like these fascinated Jastrow because he believed they showed how culture, context, and previous knowledge and experience all influence what we perceive.

To illustrate what he meant, Jastrow used a duck-rabbit illustration, a so-called "ambiguous figure" that invites two or more distinct perceptions, both of which are correct but only one of which can be seen at a time.

When seen as a rabbit, the face is turned to the right, with the long ears streaming out behind. When seen as a duck, the face is turned to the left, with the ears transformed into a half-opened bill.

Rabbit or duck, but not both at once

Ambiguous figures like the duck-rabbit image reveal, according to Jastrow, that

> Seeing is not wholly an objective matter depending upon what there is to be seen, but is very considerably a subjective matter depending upon the eye that sees.
>
> —JOSEPH JASTROW

Indeed, children shown the duck-rabbit image around Easter tend to see a rabbit; those shown the image at other times tend to see a duck.

Seeing double is one of the signature techniques of visual wit.

One of the earliest expressions of this kind of "seeing as seeming" in art history can be found in trompe l'oeil paintings of the sixteenth century, in which the work is intended to seem as real—or realer—than the thing itself.

Legend has it that Zeuxis and Parrhasius, two ancient Greek painters, were competing for the honor of greatest living artist. Zeuxis's entry was a bunch of grapes painted with such verisimilitude that birds alighted on the canvas to peck at them. Parrhasius's effort, a lush floral still life, was partially concealed behind a curtain, but when Zeuxis went to pull aside the curtain he discovered that the curtain, too, was painted.

Parrhasius won the contest.

In the sixteenth century, Italian artist Giuseppe Arcimboldo continued the trompe l'oeil tradition, creating bizarre portraiture composed of objects related to the profession of the subject— a gardener painted out of vegetables, a librarian painted out of books, and, as you see here, an admiral painted out of fish.

Giuseppe Arcimboldo's *The Admiral*

Arcimboldo's portrait is a kind of ambiguous figure. Looked at one way it's a not very realistic likeness of a person; looked at another way it's a crisp trompe l'oeil rendering of selected fish and crustaceans. Unlike the duck-rabbit image, you can see *The Admiral* (circa 1560s) at once as both fish and face. In this respect, the piece is an elaborate visual pun, placing in the mind two different images of the same thing at the same time.

Verbal puns require listeners to juggle double meanings; optical ones require viewers to juggle double vision.

Marcel Mariën, another artist who enjoyed working with marine life, was an accomplished visual punster.

Mariën started out as a photographer's apprentice while still in his teens. But in 1935, after seeing the work of René Magritte for the first time, he decided on a career as an artist, soon becoming a close friend of Magritte and one of the most prominent of the Belgian Surrealists. He worked in a variety of media—photography, film, collage, and "ready-mades," works of art assembled from discarded materials, common household items, or unused parts of other objects.

Mariën's work shows his mischievous sense of wit, often expressed by stripping everyday things of their standard forms or functions and presenting them in a defamiliarized context, as Shklovsky's theory would have it.

In *The Tao* (1976), a toy cyclist rides along the edge of a knife; in *Crime and Reward* (1975), an ax sprouts branches from its shaft; in *The Unfindable* (1937), cyclopean spectacles sport just a single lens, a piece Mariën is said to have made after his glasses snapped in half.

In *Star Dancer* (1991), shown here, Mariën attached a doll's high-heel shoe to one of the arms of a dead starfish, transforming it into a wispy Matisse-like ballerina. The strange juxtaposition makes the viewer do a double take. How can such a clearly alien creature have such distinctly human expressiveness?

Marcel Mariën's *Star Dancer*

Mariën is said to have once remarked to a friend:

> Have you ever been alive?
> Curious sensation, isn't it?
> —MARCEL MARIËN

That "curious sensation"—that moment of "defamiliarization" in which the object is not one thing or the other, neither starfish nor dancer, but both things at once—is where visual wit lives.

Often the artist creates this uncanny evocation of oddity and familiarity through the slightest of tweaks, the lightest of touches, like slipping a high-heel shoe onto a starfish—or by gently bending to aesthetic purposes odds and ends collected from daily life.

Swiss artist Markus Raetz has a Jastrow-like fascination with the nature of human perception and how the viewer's perspective influences what is seen. Born near Bern, Raetz initially worked as a primary school teacher to fund his artistic practice, which includes drawing, photography, painting, and sculpture made from found materials, such as pieces of wood, metal, and cardboard, as well as leaves and twigs. Raetz created one series of finely crafted minimalist portraits, including two swimmers whose faces are partially submerged in water, entirely from strategically placed eucalyptus leaves.

Raetz's *EVA* (1970)—there it is there—is a remarkable rendering of a female nude made from nothing more than artfully arranged elm branches set in Plasticine.

EVA by Markus Raetz

Raetz's method, as well as that of Mariën, is reminiscent of the *bricoleur*, who sees in odds and ends, scraps and rejects, and other inauspicious materials the makings of works of art. *Bricoleurs* put into artistic practice Jastrow's insight that seeing is a mental act, not just a visual one. By plucking an object from its familiar setting and displaying it slightly awry, off-kilter, or askew, they make us see even the most ordinary objects as things entirely new.

In art, anamorphoses, images or projections whose full aspect can only be taken in from a single vantage point, are perhaps the most extreme examples of how the viewer's point of view determines what is seen—or if anything is seen at all.

Raetz makes amusing anamorphoses, such as *Yes-No* (2003), a sculpture that displays the words "yes" or "no" depending on the position of the viewer. He also makes large outdoor works that resemble piles of abandoned building material, until from a specific angle they reveal themselves to be giant reclining stick figures, one with its head gently resting on a forearm, another with its hands cupped behind its neck to make a pillow. One seemingly random jumble of concrete pilings scattered across a field in Basel's Merian Park can only be seen as a face from a certain spot on a nearby hill.

Japanese graphic designer Shigeo Fukuda was another artist fond of anamorphoses.

Fukuda was a visual trickster. He built a brick wall out of rubber that included a hidden seam through which visitors could squeeze, allowing them to pass freely through an apparently solid object. His *Victory 1945* anti-war poster (1975) depicts an artillery shell that has reversed course, hurtling back toward the barrel of the howitzer from which it has been fired. Fukuda's work combines the optical allusiveness of M. C. Escher (another anti-war poster shows a repeating pattern of handguns gradually morph into peace signs) with the prankishness of the Surrealists. (Exploiting an illusion of perspective, he fooled visitors to his home on the outskirts of Tokyo into thinking the front door was where it was not.)

Some of Fukuda's wittiest creations are anamorphic shadow art, which resemble chaotic collections of *bricoleur*-like bric-a-brac—until you view the shadow cast when the work is lit from a specific angle. *The Sea Cannot Be Cut Apart* (1988) is a crazy heap of more than 2,000 pairs of scissors, but its shadow is a perfect replica of the sleek Japanese galleon *Nippon Maru. Lunch with a Helmet On* (1987) is composed of 848 kitchen utensils, but its shadow is a Harley-Davidson motorcycle. *Aquarium for Swimming Characters* (1988) is a mobile of corrugated fish sculptures, but their shadows spell out the names of the fish in Japanese script.

In *Underground Piano* (1984)—right there—Fukuda deconstructed a baby grand in such a way that, when seen from the right angle in a mirror, it appears miraculously intact.

Fukuda's works are real-life Jastrow illusions. They play practical jokes on the visual system, making us question where the border lies between illusion and reality—and whether we can even believe our own eyes.

Shigeo Fukuda's dual piano

Like Fukuda and Raetz, British-American artist Lenka Clayton also plays with Jastrow's idea of seeing as a double process.

Clayton's work is a ludic and eclectic mix of found material (*63 Objects Taken from My Son's Mouth*, 2011–2012, is a booklet of photos including, among other items, an acorn, bolt, Christmas decoration, cigarette butt, little wooden man, Metro ticket, sponge animal, small rocks, and American, British, and European coins extracted from her son's mouth when he was between the ages of eight months and fifteen months), surrealistic humor

(*Boomerang Sent to Australia and Back Again*, 2014, is a packaged boomerang flown from Pittsburgh to Australia and Australia back to Pittsburgh via airmail), and community projects (in *Local Newspaper*, 2007, she searched for and attempted to contact all 613 people mentioned in a single edition of the local German weekly, *Wilhelmsburger Wochenblatt*).

In *Typewriter Drawings* (2012–ongoing) Clayton makes simple line drawings of ordinary objects—a shoe, a knitted jumper, folded towels, a brick wall, toenail clippings, a pair of glasses, intricately decorated plates and vases, a coat hanger (you see it here) among other items—on a portable 1957 Smith-Corona Skyriter typewriter.

COAT-HANGER 08/01/2015

Coat-Hanger by Lenka Clayton

Through her ongoing series of typewriter images, Clayton constructs a visual vocabulary from symbols typically used to construct a verbal one. From ampersands and asterisks, commas and quotation marks, she makes images of carpets, drinking straws, torn screen doors, and paper clips. It's a weird trompe l'oeil realm, in which, like Arcimboldo's portraits, Clayton depicts her subjects by assembling meticulous depictions of other stuff.

Unlike Arcimboldo, though, Clayton's raw material does not consist in physical objects—vegetables, books, fish—but in linguistic ones. Her alphabet spells out not the names of things, but the things themselves. Her work, quite literally, leads from word to world.

I see I've already run over my time, but in concluding my talk I wanted to leave you with the suggestion that perhaps what connects artists as distant in time, media, and style as Arcimboldo, Mariën, Raetz, Fukuda, and Clayton is a supernormal sensitivity to visual ambiguity. Their work presents us with visual experiences in which multiple interpretations are not only possible but required. The work is two things at once—a female nude *and* some bent twigs, a piano *and* an un-piano, a hanger *and* a bunch of long dashes and parentheses.

As Joseph Jastrow argued, true vision depends upon your point of view, and seeing clearly means doing a double take. That's the essence of visual wit.

Thank you very much.

WISDOM
OF THE SAGES

*Being stories of the witty life, with commentary
characteristic of the Talmud and Zen koan collections*

ONE DAY A FRIEND INVITED HERSHELE OSTROPOLER to his home for lunch. The friend ordered two loaves of bread from the bakery and asked Hershele to pick them up on his way. Hershele did so, noticing that one loaf was much smaller than the other. When Hershele arrived at his friend's house, he handed him the smaller loaf and kept the larger one for himself.

"That's very rude," his friend said.

"Really?" Hershele asked. "What would you have done in my place?"

"I would have given you the larger loaf and kept the smaller one for myself, of course!"

"Well, you've *got* the smaller one. What more do you want?"

Hershele Ostropoler lived in the late eighteenth century in the Ukrainian village of Ostropol, from where he took his surname. Legend has it that when Hershele was fired from his butcher's job because of his incessant joking, he wandered around Ukraine looking for gainful employment. He eventually stumbled into the court of Rabbi Barukh of Mezhbizh, a local religious leader who suffered from depression. Charmed by Hershele's wit, Barukh hired him as a court jester to relieve his chronic bouts of melancholy.

Stories of Hershele's wittiness have made him something of a folk hero in Eastern and Central Europe, and his ingenious reasoning recalls the scrappy, argumentative logic of the Talmud, Judaism's treatise on religious observance and ritual law, and the slapstick stories of enlightenment found in koans, the closest thing Zen Buddhism has to sacred scriptures.

Unlike other religious texts, the Talmud and the great koan collections *The Gateless Gate* and the *Blue Cliff Records* are not considered flawless, infallible, or even finished. Neither Judaism nor Buddhism have a final clerical authority, so the Talmud is an open-ended debate among rabbis about everything from God's omniscience and the creation of the world to the finer points of Jewish ethics and the interpretation of biblical texts, while koans are cryptic encounters between monks in which spiritual insight is attained—or not attained, as the case may be—through paradox and unreason.

The Talmud is more a conversation than a catechism, recording the arguments and counterarguments of the Jewish sages over a period of some seven hundred years, roughly between 200 BCE and 500 CE. Rabbis analyzed the Bible sentence by sentence, refining or rejecting the interpretations of their predecessors and adding their own exegesis. Philosophical free association rules, with rabbis refuting, rebuking, and occasionally agreeing with each other in a series of stories, commentaries, and aphorisms. The whole proceeds by dispute and digression, in no particular order, neither by chronology nor by subject matter.

The *Blue Cliff Records* and *The Gateless Gate*, compiled in China in the eleventh and thirteenth centuries, respectively, present seemingly illogical riddles designed not so much to challenge a monk's intelligence as to test his or her tolerance for ambiguity. The insolubility of a koan is an end in itself, reinforcing the Zen lesson that true understanding cannot be reached through ordinary reasoning.

The story told by Kyogen Osho, a ninth century Chinese monk, comparing enlightenment to a man up a tree is a case in point:

> Enlightenment is like a man hanging by his teeth from a branch high up in a tree. His hands grasp no bough; his feet rest on no limb. Someone appears below him and shouts, "What is the meaning of Zen?" If he does not answer, he fails to respond to the question. If he does answer, he falls and loses his life. What would you do in such a situation?

What the ancient Jewish and Chinese sages did in such situations was to keep talking, to keep arguing, and to keep amending and appending the stories told by those who came before them. They developed a methodology of sorts—sequential series of commentaries and philosophical dialogues compiled across generations—in which mind sharpens mind and wit sharpens wit.

Certain techniques recur as particularly effective:

- Take things literally that are meant figuratively.
- Place things commonly understood in one category in an entirely different category.
- Benignly violate the most pervasively held expectations.
- Deploy the ludicrous to get at the astute.
- Use practical jokes to trip up practical minds.
- Equate spiritual wisdom with common sense that meets the existential challenges of everyday life.

The logic of these tactics is impeccable, if not always conventional. And while the arguments themselves are refutable, it is the process rather than the final product that matters.

The Talmud, the *Blue Cliff Records*, and *The Gateless Gate* esteem disputation over certitude, continuous inquiry over tidy doctrinal conclusions. They contend that there is no gate to go through, no stairs to ascend. Nothing less than your direct realization is demanded. In this, this ancient form of argument and storytelling is a model and a metaphor for wit itself.

· · · ·

ONCE, AT DINNER, when Rabbi Barukh was too depressed to eat, Hershele sat down across from him and slipped a silver teaspoon into his pocket. Before Barukh could rebuke him for the theft, Hershele said, "Doctor's orders: Take a teaspoon with every meal." Barukh, smiling, recovered his appetite.

Commentary: Hershele twice takes what has not been given. First, a silver teaspoon that does not belong to him, then a literal statement in place of a metaphorical one. If wit consists, as we say, in the ability to hold in the mind two different ideas about the same thing at the same time, this is exactly the function of metaphor. A metaphor carries the attention from the concrete to the abstract, from object to concept. When that direction is reversed, and attention is brought back from concept to object, the mind is surprised. Mistaking the figurative for fact is therefore a signature trick of wit.

So it is said of Brother Groucho that, when his son was denied entry to a country club swimming pool closed to Jews, he dispatched a telegram to the establishment asking if the boy, born of a Gentile mother, could go in up to his waist since he was only half Jewish.

Rabbi Bergson called this "reciprocal interference"—when one thing "belongs simultaneously to two altogether independent series of events and is capable of being interpreted in two entirely different meanings at the same time." Causing the literal to interfere with the metaphorical makes the original act or statement appear ridiculous.

John Scogan, having greatly offended Edward IV, was on pain of death forbidden from ever again setting foot on English soil. So the royal jester fled to France, where he filled his shoes with Gallic loam and brazenly returned to court, escaping execution.

Therefore did Friar Wystan write, "One of the most fruitful devices of wit is the imaginary treatment of analogous situations as if they were identical. Metaphor (the relation by analogy) is pushed to the absurd point where it is made to appear as exact concrete description."

Here, too, Hershele instructs us. Once, during the Passover feast, he sat across from an arrogant rich man disgusted by Hershele's lack of manners. "What separates you from a pig is what I'd like to know," the man sneered.

"The table," Hershele answered.

Hence is it said, kleptomaniacs don't understand metaphor because they take things literally.

. . . . .

HAVING HIRED HARPO and Chico to dig up incriminating information on Groucho, scheming Ambassador Trentino demands to know if they have obtained Groucho's criminal record. In response, Harpo presents him with a gramophone disc. Furious, Trentino throws the record into the air, whereupon Harpo casually produces a pistol from his overcoat and blows it out of the sky like a clay skeet-shooting target.

Commentary: The ancient sages never ceased to extoll the virtues of the category mistake, an error in which a thing belonging to one category is presented or understood as belonging to another category. Brother Harpo is categorically mistaken twice in quick succession, confusing a criminal record with a phonographic record and conflating a vinyl disc with a skeet-shooting target.

Category mistakes are often committed unwittingly. Headlines like "Never Withhold Herpes Infection from Loved One" or "Include Your Children when Baking Cookies" can be presented or understood in multiple categories. But the wit's category mistakes are always deliberate.

Therefore did Reverend Dukenfield, may libations be poured upon him, in answer to the question of whether he liked children, reply, "Yes, if they are properly cooked," knowingly and willfully removing the verb "like" from the "things I enjoy being around" category and placing it in the "things I enjoy eating" category.

The wit of the category mistake, like the wit of metaphor, arises from the sudden transformation of an implicit expectation into something completely different. The sense given is not the same as the sense taken.

When Pastor Gregory was denied service at a segregated Mississippi restaurant with the words, "We don't serve colored people here," he reversed the affront, saying, "I don't eat colored people nowhere!"

Aristotle, blessings be upon him, called this ability to quickly skip from category to category *eutrapelia*, the quality of "turning easily," of being nimble-witted. The person thus endowed is able to turn the tables with a turn of phrase, a versatility much admired by the Greek philosopher: "Such sallies are believed to be movements of the character and, like bodies, characters too are judged by the way they move."

So it is said of Mathurine, beloved jester to Henry III, Henry IV, and Louis XIII, that she once accompanied a lady of the court to an audience with the king. Annoyed, the lady turned to Mathurine and snapped, "I don't like having a fool by my side."

"I don't mind," Mathurine replied.

. . . . .

WILE E. COYOTE (*Carnivorous vulgaris*) paints a picture of a road curving around a rock face and installs it where the actual road abruptly ends at the edge of a cliff. The Road Runner (*Accelleratii incredibilus*) speeds into the painting, disappearing around the corner with a "Meep! Meep!" Wile E. wanders into the road scratching his head just as a truck roars around the corner from inside the painting and flattens him. Peeling himself from the road, Wile E. sprints after the Road Runner but crashes through the canvas, lingering pitifully for a moment in the air, before plunging into the abyss.

Commentary: Scripture tells us that the sacrament of laughter, that outward and visible sign of inward and spiritual grace, is administered most religiously through the benign violation of expectations. A malign violation (*Risus malum*) occurs when our expectations are defied in ways perceived to be dangerous or threatening, as in the "jump scare" scene from a horror film in which the villain's grotesquely melted face abruptly appears, usually accompanied by a loud, unnerving sound. A benign violation (*Risus miraculum*) occurs when our expectations are defied in ways that leave the mind unsettled but well-being intact.

In his doomed pursuit of the Road Runner, Wile E. thrice benignly violates expectations, primarily those concerning the laws of physics: once when the Road Runner enters the painting, once when the truck exits the painting, and once when Wile E., unexpectedly restoring our previously reversed expectations, crashes through the painting and plunges into the abyss.

Benign violations bind sight gags to witticisms to punch lines: Each achieves its end by disrupting an encounter's or situation's customary outcome. When Sister Dorothy responds to an editor's urgent demand for overdue work with, "Too fucking busy, and vice versa," she decisively breaks from the conventions of meeting deadlines.

So it is written in the Book of Isaac that, as Abner's wife of many years lay dying, Abner did sit by her bedside, weeping and gnashing his teeth. With her last, gasping breaths, Abner's wife whispered, "Abner, my dear, there's something I must tell you."

"Not now, my love," Abner consoled. "Just try to get some rest."

"I can't," Abner's wife insisted. "I must tell you now. I was unfaithful to you, Abner, in this very house, not one month ago."

"Hush now, dearest," Abner said. "I know all about it. That's why I poisoned you."

. . . . .

"WHAT DOES IT say to you?" Rabbi Konigsberg asks a woman studying a Jackson Pollock painting at New York's Museum of Modern Art.

"It restates the negativeness of the universe," the woman says, "the hideous, lonely emptiness of existence. Nothing. The predicament of man forced to live in a barren, godless eternity like a tiny flame flickering in an immense void with nothing but waste, horror, and degradation, forming a useless, bleak straitjacket in a black, absurd cosmos."

"What are you doing Saturday night?" Rabbi Konigsberg ventures.

"Committing suicide," the woman replies.

"What about Friday night?"

Commentary: As the sacred texts have been handed down from generation to generation, still some method has been needed to understand the wisdom of the sages and their dark sayings. So the Wise Men of Chelm, blessings be upon them, perfected

Talmudic logic to take causal reasoning to its illogical extreme, thereby finding ludic truth in the ludicrous.

An angel flew out from heaven with two sacks of souls, one filled with the wise and the other filled with the foolish. Instructed to disperse the souls equally across the earth, the angel accidentally tore a hole in the sack filled with fools while flying over a mountain pass, and all those souls poured out into one place: Chelm.

When Chelmites were injuring themselves at alarming rates by falling from a treacherous mountain pass, the Wise Men decreed that a hospital be constructed at the bottom of the cliff for the comfort and care of the afflicted. When storms continually damaged the town's new sundial, the Wise Men ordained that a roof be constructed over it as protection from the elements.

So it was that the Wise Men won fame for their judiciousness and the subtle art of Talmudic logic was passed from sage to sage across the ages, even unto Rabbi Konigsberg.

There once was a man who lived in deathly fear of his footprints and his shadow. He wanted desperately to escape them but, despite everything he tried, his footprints and his shadow relentlessly pursued him. Panicked, he began running faster and faster and faster until he became utterly exhausted and dropped down dead. He did not realize that simply by lolling about in the shade and resting in quietude he could have put an end to his footprints and his shadow.

If wisdom becomes the wise, how much more so the foolish?

· · · ·

ONE DAY, IN a small town in the prefecture of Jianzhou, a man had a very precious object stolen from his home. Chen Shuku, the local magistrate, was called in to investigate. He questioned all the townsfolk but could not identify the culprit. So Chen Shuku brought a temple bell into the town square and concealed it behind a curtain, announcing that the bell could tell an innocent person from a thief. If an innocent person touched the bell, it would remain silent; if a guilty person touched the bell, it would ring out.

Chen Shuku brought the suspects before the bell and asked them to put their hands through the curtain to touch it. Unbeknownst to them, Chen Shuku had smeared the bell with ink. He carefully examined each hand as it was withdrawn from the curtain. Every hand was stained with ink except that of one man, who confessed to the crime.

Commentary: When dispositions are dark and intentions obscure, dissimulation will reveal what others wish to remain hidden.

Clamor in the east; attack in the west.

Lure your opponent onto the roof, then take away the ladder.

Set out for one destination, but arrive at another.

The best offense is a good pretense, and trickery is often the surest route to the truth.

To devise the correct approach, observe without ceasing and attend to everything in sight, even unto the smallest detail. It is as if a beneficent king, wishing to bestow his wealth among his people, said to his subjects, "Count gold pieces from now until tomorrow morning, and whatever you count shall be yours." How could anyone let their attention flag or their spirit be wearied that night! What fortunes would be lost in the time spent sleeping!

Therefore hath Rabbi Jon Bon Jovi, he of blessed memory, said, "I'll sleep when I'm dead."

And so it is told of Tokusan that he devoutly and persistently asked Ryutan about the nature of enlightenment far into night. Ryutan patiently answered each of Tokusan's questions, but at last he said, "It is late, Tokusan. Perhaps you should retire."

Tokusan stood up and made deep bows. But as he turned to go, he saw it had become too dark to find his way home.

Ryutan lit a paper candle and handed it to Tokusan. And just as Tokusan was about to take the candle, Ryutan blew it out.

· · · · ·

IN THE OLD city of Jerusalem lived a baker who baked the finest bread in all the land. Every morning the aroma of the soft, warm loaves filled the street, enticing patrons to line up outside his shop. And every morning a poor old woman stood outside, begging for coins and savoring the delicious smell.

One day, the baker demanded that the woman pay him for smelling his bread. She protested. A crowd gathered. They finally agreed to take the dispute to King Solomon.

"You must pay for smelling the baker's bread," King Solomon decreed. "How much money do you have?"

The old woman glumly jangled the handful of pennies in her pocket.

"Baker, you have been paid," King Solomon proclaimed.

"But she didn't give me any money," the baker objected.

"But did you not hear the coins?" King Solomon asked. "The sound of her coins is payment for the smell of your bread."

Commentary: Theoretical wisdom concerns things that are as they are. Practical wisdom concerns things that can be other than they are. Wit is practical wisdom.

If one holds forth at length about wit, confusing a wealth of words for a wealth of ideas, to what may this be likened? To pitching a shovelful of fleas from place to place.

If one's mind has no peace, and one yearns to quiet it, to what may this be likened? To the monk who implored the Buddha, "I beg you, master, pacify my mind." "Very well, bring your mind here, and I will pacify it," the Buddha said. "I have searched for my mind but cannot find it," the monk confessed. "There, your mind is pacified."

If one craves wisdom but knows not where to seek it, to what may this be likened? To a carrot: the best part is buried; you must dig for it; and there are a great many asses associated with it.

Therefore, if thou seest a person of wit, get thee betimes unto her, and let thy feet wear out the steps to her door.

So is it told that a priest, an imam, and a rabbi were discussing what they would do if the Almighty sent another Great Flood to inundate the earth.

"We would pray to God to spare us," said the priest.

"We would accept the will of Allah," said the imam.

"We would learn to live underwater," said the rabbi.

The rose is obsolete.

TRUE WIT

Being a manifesto of wit's
precepts and principles

PROCLAMATION

WEARY OF THE spectacle of true wit continually obscured and displaced by the hegemony of stifling intellectual specialization and desiccated academic debate; fed up with the cultural fetishization of vapid marketing slogans, soporific sitcom quips, and all manner of spin, fraud, and snark; affronted, incensed, and incited by feckless political rhetoric and rabid partisan sound bites; and desirous of crystallizing a renewed appreciation of and predilection for spontaneous creative combustion, in which our innate and playfully transgressive intelligence, sustained by an indefatigable agility of spirit, is empowered to euthanize tired old dogmas and seize the memes of disruption, we hereby declare that . . .

1. **True wit is a way of knowing, not a foppish literary ornament.**
   Wit is the quick, instinctive, improvisational intelligence that allows us to think, say, or do the right thing at the right time in the right place.

2. **True wit is a state of mind—and a sense of humor.**

   Just as watch-makers usually provide a particularly good movement with a similarly valuable case, so it may happen with jokes that the best achievements in the way of jokes are used as an envelope for thoughts of the greatest substance.   SIGMUND FREUD

3. **True wit is brisk, frisky, promiscuous.**

   Wit is a State of Imagination [that] stands in the same Regard to Sense or Wisdom, as Lightning to the Sun, suddenly kindled and as suddenly gone.

                                         THE WEEKLY REGISTER, 1732

4. **True wit is amphibious.**

   The sign of a first-rate intelligence is the ability to hold two opposing ideas in the mind at the same time, and still retain the ability to function.   F. SCOTT FITZGERALD

5. **True wit clowns around, seriously.**

   This fellow's wise enough to play the fool / And to do that well craves a kind of wit.   WILLY THE SHAKE

6. **True wit walks a tightrope, the far end fixed to a point just out of sight.**

   We consider wit as a sort of feat or trick of intellectual dexterity, analogous, in some respects, to the extraordinary performances of jugglers and rope-dancers.

                                         DUGALD STEWART

7. **True wit speaks in conceits, connecting previously unconnected realms of information and experience.**
   What beauty is for the eyes and harmony for the ears, that the conceit is for the understanding.   BALTASAR GRACIÁN

8. **True wit makes the Word flesh so it may be spelt among us.**
   How lovely are the wiles of Words!   EMILY DICKINSON

All things are big with jest: nothing's that plain,

But may be witty, if thou hast the vein.

GEORGE HERBERT

Being a sermon on the purpose of wit

Not long ago I was driving along an old country lane in Maine when I came to a crossroads. There were two signs by the side of the road, one pointing to the left and the other pointing to the right. Both signs had the same word written on them: "Addison," the name of my destination.

My mind was sorely troubled, and I did not know which way to turn.

I saw an elderly gentleman leaning on a fence at the crossroads. So I pulled over, got out of the car, and approached him.

"Excuse me, sir," I said. "I'm a stranger here, trying to get to Addison. Does it matter which way I turn?"

The man regarded me blankly for a moment and said, "Not to me it don't."

We live our lives by signs.

Street signs tell us: "Stop," "Yield."

Door signs tell us: "Enter," "Exit."

Store signs tell us: "Open," "Closed."

Lawn signs tell us: "For Sale," "Stay on the path."

The natural world is also filled with signs. A rainbow is a sign of hope, a lightning bolt a sign of danger. A troubled sea is a sign, and so is an infant's smile.

Everywhere we look we see signs. We can't even stop to ask directions without the universe trying to tell us something through some kind of sign.

In the Bible, of course, everybody is always looking for a sign. In Exodus, Moses fears the Israelites will not hear him unless the Lord gives them a sign. In Matthew, Luke, and John, Jesus wearies of the fact that, except they see signs and wonders, people will not believe.

In the early days of Christianity, desert monks roamed around Egypt imploring one another, "Give me a word, Father, a sign, that I may be edified." Often the monk on the receiving end of this request, tired of all the looking for signs, just slammed the door in the other monk's face.

One day Abba Theophilus, the archbishop, came to Scetis. The brethren assembled there said to Abba Pambo, "Say something to the archbishop, so he may have a sign and be edified."

Abba Pambo said to them, "If he is not edified by my silence, he will not be edified by my speech."

Yea, verily, we live our lives by signs.

Now, we all come to so many crossroads in our lives. Every day, every moment of every day, is a turning point of some sort. "The bottom of the mind is paved with crossroads," French poet Paul Valéry wrote.

Standing there, considering our options, wouldn't we all dearly love to have a sign, some simple sign to reassure us about our choice? Did we pick the right course? The right career? The right spouse?

Give us some kind of sign that we may know we're on the right path.

Trouble is, with so many signs—signs that point in opposite directions, obscure signs we're not sure how to interpret—how do we know which way to turn? How do we know we're headed in the right direction? How do we even know whether we're coming or going?

Brothers and sisters, it is Wit that makes this world a skein of signs. And it is with our Wits that we unravel it.

Pray with me, if you please.

Now, there was a time, not so long ago, when we believed the universe and everything in it was one giant sign, one vast braid of correspondences. Wit so made the world that each physical object represented a metaphysical truth, and every earthly thing had its dazzling numinous ring. We could not slice an apple or split a piece of wood without finding some occult resemblance inside.

Remember, as kids, those plasma balls with the miniature, multicolored electrical storms inside? When you placed your hand on the glass, all the little lightning beams immediately started streaming toward your skin.

The world was like that, wasn't it—sizzling with spiritual energy, conducted in living color directly to your fingertips?

Well, those little lightning beams are still out there shining, still out there flashing and crackling across the universe. Baltasar Gracián, our seventeenth century Jesuit brother, called them "lines of ponderation"—the threads that connect what we see with what we mean, the paths that wind through the dark, tangled forest and into the brightest clearing, the tracks that join the farthest whistle-stops of the lone human mind to the Grand Central Station of our collective consciousness.

And we can see how these lines of ponderation bind all divided and disparate things because Wit has given us homiletic eyes—eyes that see signs and homilies in all things.

ow, when I talk about homiletics, I'm not talking about some long, tedious homily delivered in a dry, academic drone from some remote and lofty pulpit.

I'm not talking about a moralizing lecture condemning sin and praising virtue, either.

And I'm definitely not talking about the kind of sermon that stranger heard who, passing through town of a Sunday morning, slipped into the back pew of the local church to worship. When the service ended, the minister asked members of the board to stay behind for their monthly meeting. So, as the congregation filed out, the elders, deacons, and a handful of other parishioners remained seated. And so did that stranger.

"Perhaps you misunderstood," the minister said. "I asked only members of the board to stay behind."

"I've never been so bored in my life!" the stranger replied.

No, I'm not talking about that kind of homiletics.

When I talk about a homiletics, I'm talking about a homily that's homely. George Herbert, rector of a little parish church in Bemerton in southwest England, said a good sermon is like a well-stocked shop, filled with all the essentials of life but also with all the stuff folks don't yet know they need, "because people by what they understand are best led to what they understand not."

When I talk about a homiletics, I'm talking about an electrifying lecture that takes us to the "thin places" in our lives, those crossroads where the profane and the sacred, the profound and the pedestrian meet.

And I'm definitely talking about the kind of sermon that informs and inflames each and every member of the congregation, so that none goes out the same as she came in. Like the story of the disciple of a famous Sufi master who was sitting in a Baghdad café sipping tea one day when he overheard the Angel of Death chatting with an acquaintance. "I have several calls to make in this city during the next three weeks," he heard Death remark.

Terrified that Death would call on him, the disciple fled to the remote town of Samarkand on the fastest horse he could hire, reasoning that if he stayed away for the next three weeks Death could not touch him.

A few days later, Death bumped into the famous Sufi master on the street and inquired as to the whereabouts of his disciple. "Oh, he should be around here somewhere," the Sufi master said, "probably meditating."

"That's strange," Death replied, "because I'm scheduled to collect him in a couple of weeks' time—in Samarkand, of all places."

Now, we may ask ourselves, why does Wit speak to us in

signs? Why is an elderly gentleman leaning against a fence an image of the universe? Why is that plasma ball from my childhood an image of my soul? Why do we find these lines of ponderation embossed across the globe?

Well, Saint Augustine tells us, "What is attended with difficulty in the seeking gives greater pleasure in the finding." Wit has, with admirable wisdom and care for the spirit, given us divining minds that delight in making signs and homiletic eyes that delight in descrying them.

With homiletic eyes, we can see how everything is both itself and something else.

With homiletic eyes, we can see in proverbs and in parables what is particular to our own predicament.

With homiletic eyes, we can see Wit's signature in all things—the tongue in every tree, the book in every running brook, the sermon in every stone.

We come into this world with nothing, and we leave it the same way. In between, we must each awake at last alone to Wit's one true end: to begin, be glad, and be gone.

I wish I had someone to pray with me up here.

You see, the good book—*Psychological Bulletin*, vol. 134, no. 6, 2008, pages 779 through 806—tells us that we are more original and open-minded, more ingenious and inventive, more spontaneous and playful after the holy spirit of Wit visits us.

That's why Rabbah, head of the academy in ancient Babylonia, in the great city of Pumbedita, near present-day Fallujah, opened every lecture with an amusing story. So it is written in the Babylonian Talmud, "Even as Rabbah before he commenced [his discourse] before the scholars used to say something humorous, and the scholars were cheered."

That's why, in 1809, Irish playwright Richard Brinsley Sheridan calmly sipped his claret as he watched flames engulf his beloved Drury Lane Theatre, an establishment of which he was the proprietor and from which he earned his living. When a friend expressed astonishment at his serenity, he replied, "Surely, a man may be allowed to take a glass of wine by his own fireside."

That's why German theologian Reinhold Niebuhr believed "laughter is the beginning of prayer," because Wit, like faith, beholds with equanimity life and death, wealth and poverty, fame and ignominy—all the inscrutable incongruities of our mortal existence here on earth.

And, yes, my brothers and sisters, that's also why angels can fly—because they take themselves lightly!

What abides of Wit are smarts, grit, and levity, these three; but the greatest of these is levity.

Now, we may also ask ourselves, where is Wit to be found? Where must we go to seek it? And where can we reclaim our Wits when, as is as sure to happen as winter follows spring and night follows day, we lose them?

Well, it's not like in *Orlando Furioso*, where Orlando falls madly in love with Angelica and when she elopes with someone else completely loses his Wits. His friend Astolfo travels all the way to the moon, because things mislaid down here—patience, reputation, courage, time, Wit—collect up there.

Wandering through the valley of lost things, Astolfo finally reaches a mountain of brains, each "soft, tenuous liquid" sealed in an individual vial of greater or lesser size. There he finds what's he's been looking for: the biggest vial of them all, with "the Wits of Orlando" written on it.

Astolfo gathers up the Wits and restores them to his distraught and demented friend.

No, it's not like that. Wit is always nearer than we think.

No, it's more like the story of that wealthy merchant who makes a lengthy pilgrimage carrying all his most precious jewels. Along the way, another traveler befriends him but secretly means to steal his treasure.

The two pilgrims share a room at a local inn every evening, each receiving a mat and pillow, washbasin and towel. Every night before going to sleep, the merchant, being wise in the ways of the world, allows his traveling companion to use the bathroom first. While the man is making his ablutions, the merchant slips the jewels under his companion's pillow.

As soon as the merchant leaves to use the bathroom himself, the would-be thief rummages through his things, frantically searching under the merchant's mat and pillow but never finding the jewels he seeks—and never thinking to look where he lays his own head every night.

Yes, Wit is always nearer than we think. Wit is always nearer than we think.

Can I get someone to pray with me up here?

ow, you may be thinking to yourself, all this talk about "a skein of signs" and "homiletic eyes" is all well and good for folks who have reached a crossroads in their lives. But what about the folks who aren't quite there yet? What about the folks still lost in a dark wood, hacking their way through the underbrush?

You may be thinking, if you're already at a crossroads, consider yourself lucky. At least you've reached a place where you can make a choice: Turn left or turn right. Go forward or go back.

You may be thinking, after all, the most harrowing time is *before* you reach the crossroads, when you've been walking and walking and you just can't find the path, when you've been driving and driving and you have no idea if you're headed in the right direction, when you're scared and on your own a long, long way from home and you just know that elderly gentleman leaning against the fence isn't going to help.

Well, I say to you, that is so. That is true. That is why Brother Brudzinski observed, "The most difficult thing to find is the way to the signposts."

But, I also say to you, the dark is a sign, even as the light. And the want of all help is sometimes all the help we need.

One day, when I was young, lost in a dark and sign-less time, I was walking up Oak Street in San Francisco, toward Fillmore Street. My mind was troubled and cloudy. My eyes were fixed on the ground, where I was shocked to see a writhing, hissing snake on the sidewalk right in front of me. As I stood there, thrilled and fearful, it climbed into the wheel well of a parked car and disappeared.

What this thick, sinewy serpent—symbol of knowledge and wisdom—was doing in the middle of San Francisco I did not know. And seeing it did not solve any of my problems. But it did give me a desperately needed glimpse of the path ahead.

When troubles mount, Wit will figure it out.

When all hope seems gone, Wit will find a way.

When life brings you down, Wit will lift you up.

So fly high, my brothers and sisters, within the center of the storm. And when you fall, fall headlong into Wit's wide-open arms.

Find the signs that return you firmly to your right and only road. Make a joyful noise unto the void.

> If the only prayer you said in your whole life was,
>
> "Thank you," that would suffice.
>
> MEISTER ECKHART

WIT THANKS

Being what's more formally known as the
"Acknowledgments"

To write of Wit I first picked up my pen
All the way back in two thousand and ten.
To those who aided me from there to here:
"Thanks, and thanks, and ever thanks," per Shakespeare.

Early steps in this investigation
Were taken at the Nieman Foundation,
Where the fellowship, learning, and debate
Did my skills both promote and elevate.

Thank you, curators Giles and Lipinski
(The latter hired me; the former picked me),
And thank you, members of the Nieman staff,
For all you do on the fellows' behalf.

I take off my hat to Jordan Finkin,
whose Jewish humor course got me thinking.
My handle on verbal wit was far less
Until Gilad Ben-Shach taught me to fence.

James Dennen provided consultation
On that ancient art, improvisation,
While performer Paul Dome worked hard and played
To show me some of the tricks of the trade.

The late Justin Kaplan told me, bluntly,
The book's one problem: "It isn't funny."
So chapter by chapter, draft after draft,
I labored to include sufficient laughs.

I'm lucky to have insightful readers
Telling which lines were losers, which keepers.
For saying if jive was utter folly,
Grazie to Issac, Jeneé, and Lolly!

Gudrun Brug read in terms not uncertain,
Also, of course, correcting my German.
Blaine Greteman, with laudable reflection,
Commented on the Addison section.

For help with the Germaine-Denis duel
I thank my friend Mr. Michael Newell.
Christopher Weyant, whose wit's prodigious,
Gave recommendations most auspicious.

David Shields's outlook on the obstacles
Showed that the book was, in fact, possible.
Eryn Carlson, defying all strictures,
Both found the credits and sourced the pictures.

Some kind, intrepid souls read the whole book,
Not ruing, I hope, the time that it took.
Kari Howard offered key exchanges
Regarding all the stylistic changes.

Katherine Stewart, to utmost effect,
Did "destaël" the essence of the subject,
And so did Margherita Abbozzo—
brio, bravura, and furioso!

For smart suggestions, major and minor,
I am very grateful to Russ Rymer.
From the vision system to linguistics,
Justin Junge adjudged things scientific.

Chris Walsh scoured the text with a comb fine-toothed,
Fixing thoughts unclear and phrases uncouth;
Improving the text from finish to start,
Hence this thanks from the bottom of my heart.

Jill Bialosky got this idea
When others said: "Severe logorrhea."
Katinka Matson, whose counsel was sage,
Helped get the words from my head to the page.

For Linda, Gilles, Hendrikje, Tristan,
I here conclude with a quote from Wystan,
That witty twist on the poet's blessing:
Knowing is always more fun than guessing.

NOTES AND BIBLIOGRAPHY

vii **"The highest wit is wisdom at play":** Cited in Robert Bernard Martin, *The Triumph of Wit: A Study of Victorian Comic Theory* (Oxford: Clarendon Press, 1974), 43.

OFT WAS THOUGHT, AN ESSAY IN SIXTY-FOUR LINES

Works Cited

1 **"True wit is nature to advantage dress'd":** Alexander Pope, *Complete Poetical Works*, ed. Herbert Davis (Oxford: Oxford University Press, 1983), 72.
2 **guano of the wingèd mind:** "The pun is the guano of the winged mind." Victor Hugo. Cited in Walter Redfern, *Puns* (Oxford: Basil Blackwell, 1984), 141.

Works Consulted

Pope, Alexander. *Complete Poetical Works*. Edited by Herbert Davis. Oxford: Oxford University Press, 1983.

ONE BAD APPLE, OR, AN APOLOGY FOR PARONOMASIA

Works Cited

5 **"In the beginning was the pun":** Samuel Beckett, *Murphy* (New York: Grove Press, 1957), 65.
7 **the sun god Ra's tears:** Geraldine Pinch, *Magic in Ancient Egypt* (London: British Museum Press, 1994), 68.
7 **The opening verses of the ancient Indian epic the *Ramayana*:**

Gurupad K. Hegde, *Pun in Sanskrit Literature: A New Approach* (Mysore: Prasaranga, University of Mysore, 1982), 22–23.

7 **"The way (*tao*) that can be talked about (*tao*)":** Yi Wu, *The Book of Lao Tzu* (San Francisco: Great Learning, 1989), 2–3.

7 **"Of course, sir, either oar":** Walter Redfern, *Puns* (Oxford: Basil Blackwell, 1984), 127.

8 **Opposite meanings of "fast" and "cleave":** Ibid., 44–45.

8 **they speak "twice as much by being split":** Alexander Pope, "The Art of Sinking in Poetry," in *The Works of Alexander Pope Esq., In Nine Volumes Complete, with His Last Corrections, Additions, and Improvements, as They Were Delivered to the Editor a Little Before His Death, Together with the Commentary and Notes of Mr. Warburton*, vol. 6 (London, 1760), 231.

9 **the world as a place "where unexpected simultaneities are the rule":** Richard Ellmann, *James Joyce* (Oxford: Oxford University Press, 1983), 551.

9 **The average number of puns in a Shakespeare play:** M. M. Mahood, *Shakespeare's Wordplay* (London: Methuen, 1979), 164.

9 **"A quibble is the golden apple":** Samuel Johnson, "Preface to Shakespeare," in: *Poetry and Prose*, ed. Mona Wilson (Cambridge, MA: Harvard University Press, 1967), 500.

10 **in puns, ideas rhyme:** William Shakespeare, *Shakespeare's Sonnets*, ed. Stephen Booth. (New Haven, CT: Yale University Press, 1977), 371.

10 **During a stint on the circuit court in Bloomington, Illinois:** P. M. Zall, *Abe Lincoln Laughing: Humorous Anecdotes from Original Sources by and about Abraham Lincoln* (Berkeley: University of California Press, 1982), 72–73.

11 **"T. R. Strong but coffee are stronger":** Ibid., 33.

11 **"If I don't suspend it tonight":** Ibid., 113.

12 **"just as if I were his equal, quite famillionaire":** Sigmund Freud, *Jokes and Their Relationship to the Unconscious* (London: Penguin Books, 1976), 191.

12 **"the peculiar process of condensation and fusion":** Ibid., 55.

13 **"Delighted surprise is the common immediate sensation":** Isaac Tuxton, "Wit," *The Irish Monthly* 5 (1877), 341.

13 **"Whenever resemblances or relations are established":** Isaac Tuxton, cited in Robert Bernard Martin, *The Triumph of Wit: A Study of Victorian Comic Theory* (Oxford: Clarendon Press, 1974), 45.

13 **Charles Lamb's last breath:** Charles Lamb, *The Letters of Charles Lamb, In which Many Mutilated Words and Passages Have Been Restored to Their Original Form, with Letters Never Before Published*

and Facsimiles of Original Ms. Letters and Poems, vol. 3 (Boston: Bibliophile Society, 1905), 192.

13 **"I wool"**: R. H. Blyth, *Japanese Humour* (Tokyo: Japan Travel Bureau, 1957), 16.

13 **"All men who possess at once active fancy"**: Samuel Taylor Coleridge, *Marginalia*, ed. George Whalley, vol. 1 (Princeton, NJ: Princeton University Press, 2001), 610.

14 **"A ridiculous likeness"**: Ibid, 610.

14 **"two strings of thought tied together by an acoustic knot"**: Arthur Koestler, *The Art of Creation* (London: Pan Books, 1969), 65.

14 **"compels us to perceive the situation"**: Ibid., 112.

14 **Newton's and Cézanne's apples**: Ibid., 108.

15 **"Aha," "Ah," and "Ha-ha"**: Arthur Koestler, "Humor and Wit," *Janus: A Summing Up* (New York: Vintage Books, 1979), 110.

15 **"Comic discovery is paradox stated"**: Koestler, *The Art of Creation*, 96.

15 **"the conscious and unconscious processes underlying creativity"**: Koestler, "Humor and Wit," 129.

16 **"the pun is not bound by the laws"**: Charles Lamb, "That the Worst Puns Are the Best (Popular Fallacies IX)," *The Last Essays of Elia* (London: J. M. Dent, 1898), 199.

Works Consulted

Ackerley, C. J. "In The Beginning Was the Pun." *Journal of the Australasian Modern Language Association* 55 (1981): 15–22.

Barnet, Sylvan. "Coleridge on Puns: A Note to His Shakespeare Criticism." *Journal of English and Germanic Philology* 56, no. 4 (1957): 602–609.

Booth, Stephen. *An Essay on Shakespeare's Sonnets*. New Haven, CT: Yale University Press, 1969.

———— (ed.). *Shakespeare's Sonnets*. With an analytic commentary by Stephen Booth. New Haven, CT: Yale University Press, 1977.

————. *King Lear, Macbeth, Indefinition, and Tragedy*. New Haven, CT: Yale University Press, 1983.

Brown, James. "Eight Types of Pun." *Publications of the Modern Language Association of America* 71 (1956): 14–26.

Burgess, Anthony. *Joysprick: An Introduction to the Language of James Joyce*. London: Andre Deutsch, 1963.

————. *Re Joyce*. New York: W. W. Norton, 1968.

————. *Language Made Plain*. New York: Thomas Y. Crowell, 1969.

Certeau, Michel de. *The Practice of Everyday Life*. Berkeley: University of California Press, 1988.

Crosbie, John S. *Crosbie's Dictionary of Puns*. New York: Harmony Books, 1977.

Culler, Jonathan, ed. *On Puns: The Foundation of Letters*. Oxford: Basil Blackwell, 1988.

Freud, Sigmund. *Jokes and Their Relationship to the Unconscious*. London: Penguin Books, 1976.

Houlihan, Patrick F. *Wit & Humor in Ancient Egypt*. London: Rubicon, 2001.

Hughes, Patrick, and Paul Hammond. *Upon the Pun: Dual Meaning in Words and Pictures*. London: W. H. Allen, 1978.

Jones, Ewan James. *Coleridge and the Philosophy of Poetic Form*. Cambridge: Cambridge University Press, 2014.

Koestler, Arthur. *The Art of Creation*. London: Pan Books, 1969.

———. "Humor and Wit." *Janus: A Summing Up*. New York: Vintage Books, 1979.

Lamb, Charles. "That the Worst Puns Are the Best (Popular Fallacies IX)." *The Last Essays of Elia*. London: J. M. Dent, 1898.

Leca, Benedict, ed. *The World Is an Apple: The Still Lifes of Paul Cézanne*. London: Giles, 2014.

Mahood, M. M. *Shakespeare's Wordplay*. London: Methuen, 1979.

Martin, Robert Bernard. *The Triumph of Wit: A Study of Victorian Comic Theory*. Oxford: Clarendon Press, 1974.

Mercier, Vivian. *The Irish Comic Tradition*. London: Oxford University Press, 1969.

Moger, Art. *The Complete Pun Book*. Secaucus, NJ: Castle, 1979.

Noegel, Scott B. *Puns and Pundits: Word Play in the Hebrew Bible and Ancient Near Eastern Literature*. Bethesda, MD: CDL, 2000.

Pollack, John. *The Pun Also Rises: How the Humble Pun Revolutionized Language, Changed History, and Made Wordplay More Than Some Antics*. New York: Gotham Books, 2011.

Pope, Alexander. "The Art of Sinking in Poetry." *The Works of Alexander Pope Esq., In Nine Volumes Complete, with His Last Corrections, Additions, and Improvements, as They Were Delivered to the Editor a Little Before His Death, Together with the Commentary and Notes of Mr. Warburton*, vol. 6. London, 1760.

Redfern, Walter. *Puns*. Oxford: Basil Blackwell, 1984.

Scherzer, Joel. "Oh! That's A Pun and I Didn't Mean It." *Semiotica* 22, no. 3/4 (1978): 336–350.

Swift, Jonathan. "A Modest Defence of Punning." In *The Prose Works of Jonathan Swift*, ed. Herbert Davis, vol. 4 (Oxford: Blackwell/Shakespeare Head Press, 1957), 203–210.

Untermeyer, Louis. *The Lowest Form of Wit*. New York: For the friends of George and Helen Macy, Christmas 1947.

West, Michael. *Transcendental Wordplay: America's Romantic Punsters and the Search for the Language of Nature*. Athens: Ohio University Press, 2000.

White, Roger M. *The Structure of Metaphor: The Way the Language of Metaphor Works*. Cambridge, MA: Blackwell, 1996.

THIRTY-FIVE DAYS IN MAY

Works Cited

17 **"Nothing is so much admired":** Joseph Addison, *The Spectator: With Notes, and a General Index, the Eight Volumes Comprised in One* (Philadelphia: Hickman and Hazzard, 1822), 68.

18 **The man of sensibility, like me:** Denis Diderot, "The Paradox of the Actor," in *Selected Writings on Art and Literature*, trans. Geoffrey Bremner (London: Penguin Classics, 1994), 121.

18 **That's the difference between plays and real life:** Tom Stoppard, *The Real Thing* (London: Faber and Faber, 1988), 22.

18 **for my part, I confess:** Richard Brinsley Sheridan, *The School for Scandal* (New York: Dover, 1991), 4.

18 **Pshaw! . . . the barb that makes it stick:** Ibid., 5.

19 **"a sparkling exchange of wits":** Aldo Nadi, *On Fencing* (New York: G. P. Putnam's Sons, 1943), 8.

19 **"To win":** Ibid., 14.

20 **Your touch must be felt before it is seen:** Ibid., 51.

20 **"Float like a butterfly":** A poem composed by Muhammad Ali on the occasion of his bout against George Foreman in 1974.

20 **Conception and execution must be simultaneous:** Nadi, 11.

20 **a pungent remark:** Baldesar Castiglione, *The Book of The Courtier*. trans. and with an introduction by George Bull (London: Penguin Books, 2003), 152.

21 **"to strike suddenly":** Nadi, 155.

21 **a certain nonchalance, so as to conceal all art:** Castiglione, 32.

22 **"Those are very elegant which depend":** Ibid., 167.

22 **Once, a Plains Indian had just placed:** John Morreall, *Taking Laughter Seriously* (Albany: State University of New York, 1983), 61–62.

22 **"consists in a certain dissimulation":** Castiglione, 287.

22 **Jean Harlow and Lady Margot Asquith:** Arthur Koestler, *The Art of Creation* (London: Pan Books, 1969), 50. For more information on this exchange, see the Quote Investigator website.

23 **"very short"**: Castiglione, 263–264.

23 **"Yeah, yeah"**: Hershey H. Friedman and Linda Weiser Friedman, *God Laughed: Sources of Jewish Humor* (New Brunswick, NJ: Transaction, 2014), 63.

23 **"occurs when we expect to hear one thing"**: Castiglione, 166–167.

24 **"I will not make age an issue of this campaign"**: My thanks to David Shields for suggesting the relevance of this anecdote to wit.

24 **Reagan's dead wire incident:** Gary Wills, *Reagan's America: Innocents at Home* (London: William Heinemann, 1988), 119.

25 **the lowest form of wit:** Responding to the charge that the pun was the lowest form of wit, eighteenth century Scottish lawyer Henry Erskine said, "Therefore the pun is the foundation of all wit." Cited in: Redfern, 7–8.

25 **"Your Majesty is not a subject"**: Georges de Bievre, *Calembours et Autres Jeux sur les Mots d'Esprit* (Paris: Editions Payot & Rivages, 2000), 7. My thanks to Linda Hoetink for translation from the French.

26 **There were similar verse competitions in ancient Greece:** Ernst Robert Curtius, *European Literature and the Latin Middle Ages* (New York: Harper & Row, 1963), 58.

27 **"hippocrite"**: Art Moger, *The Complete Pun Book* (Secaucus, NJ: Castle, 1979), 25.

29 **"the forming of associative elements into new combinations"**: S. A. Mednick, "The Associative Basis of the Creative Process," *Psychological Review* 69, 1962: 220–232.

29 **"Marx spots the ex"**: Cited in: Paul Hammond and Patrick Hughes, *Upon the Pun: Dual Meaning in Words and Pictures* (London: W. H. Allen, 1978), 56.

29 **"leaf" associations adapted from:** Shelley Carson, *Your Creative Brain: Seven Steps to Maximize Imagination, Productivity, and Innovation in Your Life* (San Francisco: Jossey-Bass, 2012), 136–137.

31 **"To penetrate a thought"**: Cited in: James Geary, *Geary's Guide to the World's Great Aphorists* (New York: Bloomsbury, 2007), 339.

32 **"A thought is a thing"**: Ibid., 339.

32 **Zhou Yongkang's nicknames:** Anne Henochowicz, "Eluding the Ministry of Truth," *Nieman Reports* (68)1, Winter 2014: 22–23.

34 **an instrument one likes to play:** A quote from Madame de Staël. Cited in: J. Christopher Herold, *Mistress to an Age: A Life of Madame de Staël* (Indianapolis: Bobbs-Merrill, 1958), 71.

34 **be at a loss to say something that is good and well suited:** Castiglione, 262–263.

34 **Why, are you coming apart?** Groucho Marx says this in *A Night in Casablanca.*

Works Consulted

Agrippa, Camillo. *Fencing: A Renaissance Treatise.* Translated and with an introduction by Ken Mondschein. New York: Ithaca, 2009.

Angelo, Domenico. *The School of Fencing, with a General Explanation of the Principal Attitudes and Positions Peculiar to the Art.* Edited and presented by Jared Kirby. Notes by Meastro Jeanette Acosta-Martinez. London: Greenhill Books, 2005.

Castiglione, Baldesar. *The Book of the Courtier.* Translated and with an introduction by George Bull. London: Penguin Books, 2003.

de Bievre, Georges. *Calembours et Autres Jeux sur les Mots d'Esprit.* Paris: Editions Payot & Rivages, 2000.

Diderot, Denis. "The Paradox of the Actor." In: *Selected Writings on Art and Literature.* Translated by Geoffrey Bremner. London: Penguin Classics, 1994.

Edson, Margaret. *Wit.* London: Nick Hern Books, 2011.

Goodchilds, Jacqueline D. "Effects of Being Witty on Position in the Social Structure of a Small Group." *Sociometry* (22)3, September 1959: 261–272.

———. "On Being Witty: Causes, Correlates, and Consequences." In: *The Psychology of Humor: Theoretical Perspectives and Empirical Issues.* Goldstein, Jeffrey H. and Paul E. McGhee (eds.). New York: Academic Press, 1972, 173–193.

Goodchilds, Jacqueline D., and Ewart E. Smith. "The Wit in Small and Large Established Groups." *Psychological Reports* 13, 1963: 273–274.

———. "The Wit and His Group." *Human Relations* (17)23, 1964: 3–17.

Herold, J. Christopher. *Mistress to an Age: A Life of Madame de Staël.* Indianapolis: Bobbs-Merrill, 1958.

Link, Perry. *An Anatomy of Chinese: Rhythm, Metaphor, Politics.* Cambridge, MA: Harvard University Press, 2013.

Mednick, S. A. "The Associative Basis of The Creative Process." *Psychological Review* 69, 1962: 220–232.

———. "Continual Association and Function of Level of Creativity and Type of Verbal Stimulus." *Journal of Abnormal and Social Psychology* 69(5), 1964: 511–515.

Moncrif, François Augustin de. *Art of Pleasing: An Essay on the Necessity and the Means of Pleasing.* Translated from the French of Moncrif by David E. Warden. Kingston, NY: J. Buel, 1812.

Nadi, Aldo. *On Fencing.* New York: G. P. Putnam's Sons, 1943.

Pearson, Hesketh. *Lives of the Wits*. London: Heinemann, 1962.

Sheridan, Richard Brinsley. *The School for Scandal*. New York: Dover, 1991.

Speroni, Charles. *Wit and Wisdom of the Italian Renaissance*. Berkeley and Los Angeles: University of California Press, 1964.

Tornius, Valerian. *The Salon: Its Rise and Fall, Pictures of Society through Five Centuries*. London: Thornton Butterworth, 1929.

WATCHERS AT THE GATES OF MIND: WIT AND ITS RELATION TO *WITZELSUCHT*, MALAPROPISMS, AND BIPOLAR DISORDER

Works Consulted

Carson, Shelley. "Latent Inhibition and Creativity." In: *Latent Inhibition: Cognition, Neuroscience and Applications to Schizophrenia*. Robert Lubow and Ina Weiner, eds. Cambridge: Cambridge University Press, 2010, 183–198.

————. *Your Creative Brain: Seven Steps to Maximize Imagination, Productivity, and Innovation in Your Life*. San Francisco: Jossey-Bass, 2010.

Dietrich, Arne, et al. "The Cognitive Neuroscience of Creativity." *Psychonomic Bulletin & Review* 11(6), 2004: 1011–1026.

Freud, Sigmund. *The Interpretation of Dreams*. With introduction by A. A. Brill. New York: Macmillan, 1913.

Howard-Jones, Paul A., et al. "Semantic Divergence and Creative Story Generation: An fMRI Investigation." *Cognitive Brain Research* 25, 2005: 240–250.

Peters, Gary. *The Philosophy of Improvisation*. Chicago: University of Chicago Press, 2009.

PERFECT WITTY EXPRESSIONS AND HOW TO MAKE THEM

Works Cited

52 **"Wit lies in recognizing the resemblance":** Cited in: Geary, 139.

52 **"to enliven morality with wit, and to temper wit with morality":** Joseph Addison, *The Works of Joseph Addison*, vol. 1 (New York: Harper & Brothers, 1837), 31.

52 **Given that no modern author I know of:** Addison, *Spectator*, 68.

53 **"A subject which will not bear raillery":** Anthony Ashley Cooper, Third Earl of Shaftesbury, "Sensus Communis: An Essay on the Freedom of Wit and Humor," in *Characteristics of Men, Manners,*

Opinions, Times: With a Collection of Letters, vol. 1 (London: J. J. Tournisen and J. L. Legrand, 1790), 61–62.

53 **as one who, examining individual stones from a great cathedral:** "Some who make an objection are taking a single stone from the cathedral, and finding it is nothing special." Bert Hellinger. Cited in: Geary, 238.

53 **"True wit consists in the resemblance of ideas":** Addison, *Spectator*, 74.

54 **"Not only the resemblance but the opposition of ideas":** Ibid., 74.

55 **lies "most in the assemblage of ideas":** John Locke, *Essay Concerning Human Understanding*, vol. 2 (London: Penguin Classics, 1998), xi, 2.

56 **his lover's breast is as white as snow:** Addison, *Spectator*, 74.

56 **"It is necessary that the ideas should not lie":** Ibid., 74.

56 **"Then all your beauties will be no more worth":** John Donne, *The Complete English Poems* (London: Penguin Classics, 1996), 91.

57 **"great mother of all witty expressions":** Emanuele Tesauro, *The Aristotelian Telescope*, in Dooley, Brendan (ed.). *Italy in the Baroque: Selected Readings* (New York: Garland, 1995), 463.

57 **"connects or divides them":** Ibid., 463.

58 **"packs the objects tightly together":** Ibid., 480.

59 **"sketched rather than finished":** Ibid., 462.

59 **"One object rapturously illuminated by another":** Ibid., 480.

60 **"very glittering little twigs":** From "Concerning the New Method of Investigating the Nature and Movement of Electric Fluid," contained in Appendix A of a master's thesis by Mark A. Payrebrune ("Experimental Morphology of Lichtenberg Figures," McGill University, Montreal, Canada, 1979). Dr. J. Blain of the Classics Department at McGill University translated the document.

60 **"desire of human minds to learn new things":** Tesauro, *The Aristotelian Telescope*, 474.

61 **"the most perfect witty expressions":** Ibid., 486.

61 **"mute things speak":** Ibid., 461.

Works Consulted

Addison, Joseph. *The Works of Joseph Addison*, vol. 1. New York: Harper & Brothers, 1837.

———. *The Spectator: With Notes, and a General Index, The Eight Volumes Comprised in One*. Philadelphia: Hickman and Hazzard, 1822.

Alvarez, A. *The School of Donne*. New York: Mentor Books, 1967.

Bergler, Edmund. *Laughter and the Sense of Humor*. New York: Intercontinental Medical, 1956.

Bethell, S. L. "The Nature of Metaphysical Wit." In: *Discussions of John Donne*. Frank Kermode, ed. Boston: D. C. Heath, 1962, 136–149.

Dooley, Brendan (ed.). *Italy in the Baroque: Selected Readings*. New York: Garland, 1995.

Donne, John. *The Complete English Poems*. London: Penguin Books, 1996.

Eliot, T. S. "The Metaphysical Poets." In: Kermode, 42–47.

Errett, Benjamin. *Elements of Wit: Mastering The Art of Being Interesting*. New York: Perigree, 2014.

Grierson, H. J. C. and Bullough, G. (eds.). *The Oxford Book of Seventeenth Century Verse*. Oxford: Clarendon Press, 1934.

Hazlitt, William. *Lectures on the English Comic Writers with Miscellaneous Essays*. London: J. M. Dent & Sons, 1913.

Huizinga, Johan. *Homo Ludens*. Boston: Beacon Press, 1955.

Kenner, Hugh (ed.). *Seventeenth Century Poetry: The Schools of Donne and Jonson*. New York: Holt, Rinehart and Winston, 1964.

Kermode, Frank (ed.). *Discussions of John Donne*. Boston: D. C. Heath, 1962.

Leavis, F. R. "The Line of Wit." In: *Revaluation: Tradition and Development in English Poetry*. New York: W. W. Norton, 1963.

Leishman, J. B. *The Monarch of Wit: An Analytical and Comparative Study of the Poetry of John Donne*. London: Hutchinson, 1969.

Lyly, John. *Euphues, or The Anatomy of Wit* and *Euphues and His England*. Morris William Croll and Harry Clemons, eds. New York: Russell & Russell, 1964.

Martin, Robert Bernard. *The Triumph of Wit: A Study of Victorian Comic Theory*. Oxford: Clarendon Press, 1974.

Milburn, D. Judson. *The Age of Wit, 1650–1750*. New York: Macmillan, 1966.

Sharp, Robert Lathrop. *From Donne to Dryden: The Revolt against Metaphysical Poetry*. Hamden, CT: Archon Books, 1965.

Smith, A. J. *Metaphysical Wit*. Cambridge: Cambridge University Press, 1991.

Speroni, Charles. *Wit and Wisdom of the Italian Renaissance*. Berkeley and Los Angeles: University of California Press, 1964.

Spingarn, J. E. *Critical Essays of the Seventeenth Century*, Volumes I–III. Bloomington: Indiana University Press, 1968.

Tesauro, Emanuele. *The Aristotelian Telescope*, in Dooley, Brendan (ed.). *Italy in the Baroque: Selected Readings*. New York: Garland, 1995, 460–486.

Wilcox, Helen. *"Catching the Sense": The Wit of Seventeenth-Century English Poetry*. Groningen: Phoenix, 1992.

Willey, Basil. *The Seventeenth-Century Background: Studies in the Thought of the Age in Relation to Poetry and Religion*. London: Penguin, 1962.

Williamson, George. *The Donne Tradition: Study in English Poetry from Donne to the Death of Cowley*. New York: Farrar, Straus and Cudahy, 1958.

————. *The Proper Wit of Poetry*. Chicago: University of Chicago Press, 1961.

ADVANCED BANTER

Works Cited

62 **"Jive is language in motion":** Dan Burley, *Dan Burley's Jive* (DeKalb, IL: Northern Illinois University Press, 2009), 15.

62 **Advanced Banter:** Title taken from John Lloyd and John Mitchinson, *Advanced Banter: The QI Book of Quotations* (London: Faber & Faber, 2008).

62 **beginning with a section composed in jive:** *Dan Burley's Jive* and Lavada Durst's *The Jives of Dr. Hepcat* were used in writing the jive section of this chapter.

63 **" 'Twas the dim before Nicktide":** Burley, 29.

64 **"I stash me down to cop a nod":** David Isay, *Holding On: Dreamers, Visionaries, Eccentrics, and Other American Heroes* (New York: W. W. Norton, 1996), 180.

65 **"Everyone knows that life isn't half as thrilling":** Burley, 55.

65 **"to give students of Jive":** Ibid., 11.

66 **"a satire on the conventional ofay's":** Mezz Mezzrow and Bernard Wolfe, *Really the Blues* (London: Souvenir Press, 1988), 227–228.

67 **"The Monkey and the Lion got to talkin' one day":** Daryl Cumber Dance (ed.), *From My People: 400 Years of African American Folklore* (New York: W. W. Norton & Company, 2002), 492–493.

67 **"The idea right smack in the middle of every cat's mind":** Mezzrow, 224.

67 **"On The Corner the idea":** Ibid., 226.

68 **In medieval Spain, wandering scholar-minstrels:** John H. Towsen, *Clowns* (New York: Hawthorn), 1976, 45.

68 ***Ikocha Nkocha*:** "The Dozens: An African-Heritage Theory," *Journal of Black Studies* 6(4), 1976: 401–420.

68 **whose name may come from an old English verb:** Lewis Hyde, *Trickster Makes This World: Mischief, Myth and Art* (New York: Farrar, Straus and Giroux, 2010), 273.

68 **"Your mother's like a doorknob":** This and many other wonderful Dozens slurs can be found in Mel Watkins, *African American Humor:*

The Best Black Comedy from Slavery to Today (Chicago: Lawrence Hill Books, 2002), 303–306.

69 **"I learned to talk in the street":** H. Rap Brown, *Die Nigger Die! A Political Autobiography* (Chicago: Lawrence Hill Books, 2002), 25–26.

69 **"We played the Dozens for recreation":** Ibid., 26.

70 **"suffer to be interlaced":** David Wiles, *Shakespeare's Clown: Actor and Text in the Elizabethan Playhouse* (Cambridge: Cambridge University Press, 1987), 14.

70 **when he has Hamlet describe the dead court jester Yorick:** Towsen, 58.

71 **"Methinks it is a thing unfit":** Wiles, 16.

71 **"educated insolence":** Aristotle. *Rhetoric* II, 12.

Works Consulted

Albert, Ethel M. "Culture Patterning of Speech Behavior in Burundi." In: Gumperz, John J., and D. Hymes (eds.). *Directions in Sociolinguistics*. New York: Holt, Rinehart & Winston, 1972, 72–105.

Beatty, Paul. *Hokum: An Anthology of African-American Humor*. New York: Bloomsbury, 2006.

Brown, H. Rap. *Die Nigger Die! A Political Autobiography*. Chicago: Lawrence Hill Books, 2002.

Burley, Dan. *Dan Burley's Jive*. DeKalb: Northern Illinois University Press, 2009.

Clark, Andrew (ed.). *Riffs & Choruses: A New Jazz Anthology*. London: Continuum, 2001.

DeSalvo, Debra. *The Language of the Blues, from Alcorub to Zuzu*. New York: Billboard Books, 2006.

Dillon, John, and Tania Gergel (trans.). *The Greek Sophists*. London: Penguin, 2003.

Dundes, Alan (ed.). *Mother Wit from the Laughing Barrel: Readings in the Interpretation of Afro-American Folklore*. New York: Garland, 1981.

Durst, Lavada. *The Jives of Dr. Hepcat*. Austin, TX: Self-published, 1953.

Gates, Jr., Henry Louis. *The Signifying Monkey: A Theory of African-American Literary Criticism*. New York: Oxford University Press, 1988.

Hurston, Zora Neale. "Characteristics of Negro Expression." In: *Sweat*. Wall, Cheryl A. (ed.). New Brunswick, NJ: Rutgers University Press, 1997, 55–72.

Jones, Papa Jo. *Rifftide: The Life and Opinions of Papa Jo Jones, as Told to Albert Murray*. Minneapolis: University of Minnesota Press, 2011.

Labov, William. "Rules for Ritual Insults." In: *Studies in Social Interaction*. Sudnow, David (ed.). New York: Free Press, 1972, 120–169.

Mezzrow, Mezz, and Bernard Wolfe. *Really the Blues*. London: Souvenir Press, 1988.

Towsen, John H. *Clowns*. New York: Hawthorn Books, 1976.

Tracy, Steven C. (ed.). *Writers of the Black Chicago Renaissance*. Champaign: University of Illinois Press, 2012.

Wald, Elijah. *The Dozens: A History of Rap's Mama*. Oxford: Oxford University Press, 2012.

Watkins, Mel. *African American Humor: The Best Black Comedy from Slavery to Today*. Chicago: Lawrence Hill Books, 2002.

Welsford, Enid. *The Fool: His Social and Literary History*. Garden City, NY: Anchor Books, 1961.

Wiles, David. *Shakespeare's Clown: Actor and Text in the Elizabethan Playhouse*. Cambridge: Cambridge University Press, 1987.

AN ODE TO WIT

Works Cited

76 **"If a man had time to study the history"**: C. S. Lewis, *Studies in Words* (Cambridge: Cambridge University Press, 1990), 86.

76 **Tell me, O tell, what kind of thing is wit?:** This is the first line of the ode "Of Wit" by the metaphysical poet Abraham Cowley (1618–1667).

76 **the best words in their best order:** Samuel Taylor Coleridge's (1772–1834) "homely definitions" of prose and poetry were—prose: "words in their best order"; poetry: "the best words in their best order."

Works Consulted

Darby, Derrick, and Shelby, Tommie (eds.). *Hip Hop and Philosophy*. Chicago: Open Court, 2005.

Edwards, Paul. *How to Rap: The Art and Science of the Hip-Hop MC*. Chicago: Chicago Review Press, 2009.

Lewis, C. S. *Studies in Words*. Cambridge: Cambridge University Press, 1990.

Smitherman, Geneva. *Talkin and Testifyin: The Language of Black America*. Boston: Houghton Mifflin, 1977.

TURNING WORDS

Works Cited

79 **"Turn it and turn it, for everything is in it":** Judah Goldin, *The Living Talmud: The Wisdom of the Fathers and Its Classical Commentaries, Selected and Translated with an Essay by Judah Goldin* (New York: New American Library, 1957), 223.

79 **kake-kotoba:** Robert Hass, *The Essential Haiku: Versions of Basho, Buson & Issa* (New York: Ecco, 1994), 312.

80 **full of "good turns":** *Cited in* Hugo Rahner, *Man at Play* (New York: Herder and Herder, 1972), 94.

80 **Various inquiries from growers came:** William Crocker and Lee I. Knight, "Effect of Illuminating Gas and Ethylene upon Flowering Carnations." *Botanical Gazette* 46(4), 1908: 259–276.

81 **"The most heterogeneous ideas are yoked":** Cited in Kermode, 7.

81 **the "right true end" of love:** Donne, 122.

82 **Tenali Rama attended a royal feast:** A. K. Ramanujan, *Folktales from India: A Selection of Oral Tales from Twenty-two Languages* (New York: Pantheon Books, 1991), 206.

82 **The Anang of Nigeria:** Peter Farb, *Word Play: What Happens when People Talk* (New York: Bantam Books, 1983), 143.

83 **When the Moghul emperor Akbar drew a line:** Ramanujan, 94.

83 **One day an old man lost his only horse:** Adapted from George Kao, *Chinese Wit and Humor* (New York: Coward-McCann, 1946), 32.

84 **Yang Saon's sijo:** Adapted from Richard Rutt, *The Bamboo Grove: An Introduction to Sijo* (Ann Arbor: University of Michigan Press, 1998), 20.

85 **German Lieutenant General Hermann B. von Ramcke holed up in Brest:** Jack Kneece, *Ghost Army of World War II* (Gretna, LA: Pelican, 2001), 11–14.

86 **A cabbie who successfully masters "The Knowledge":** E. A. Maguire, K. Woollett, and H. J. Spiers, "London Taxi Drivers and Bus Drivers: A Structural MRI and Neuropsychological Analysis." *Hippocampus* 16(12), 2006: 1091–1101; E. A. Maguire and K. Woollett. "Acquiring 'the Knowledge' of London's Layout Drives Structural Brain Changes," *Current Biology* 21(24–2), 2011: 2109–2114.

86 **"Attention and effort are":** William James, *The Heart of William James*, edited and with an introduction by Robert Richardson (Cambridge, MA: Harvard University Press, 2010), 113.

86 **"Keep the faculty of effort alive":** Ibid., 114.

86 **In April of 1985, the crew of the space shuttle:** John Towsen, "Zen and the Heart of Physical Comedy: The Revenge of Murphy's Law." *Theater*, Summer/Fall 1987, 21–29.

87 **As Buster Keaton settles down on a bench:** This is a scene from *The High Sign*, 1921.

87 **Keaton, a stockbroker on the verge:** This is a scene from *Seven Chances*, 1925.

87 **"Cut the cards" . . . Harpo and Chico elude the ship's onboard**

detectives: These are scenes from *Horse Feathers* and *A Day at the Races*, respectively.

88 **When the god Kareya created the world:** Richard Erdoes and Alfonso Ortiz (eds)., *American Indian Myths and Legends* (New York: Pantheon Books, 1984), 382–383.

89 **One night, amid the alarms:** Adapted from Lo Kuan-chung, *Three Kingdoms: China's Epic Drama*, translated from the Chinese and edited by Moss Roberts (New York: Pantheon Books, 1976), 294–295.

89 **"like something that had gotten loose from Macy's":** Harpo Marx, with Rowland Barber, *Harpo Speaks* (New York: Limelight Editions, 1985), 169.

90 **Wit's End:** Robert E. Drennan (ed.), *The Algonquin Wits* (New York: Citadel, 1968), 36–37.

Works Consulted

Bryant, Mark. *Riddles, Ancient & Modern*. London: Hutchinson, 1983.

Drennan, Robert E., ed. *The Algonquin Wits*. New York: Citadel, 1968.

Farb, Peter. *Word Play: What Happens when People Talk*. New York: Bantam Books, 1983.

Halpern, Charna, Del Close, and Kim Johnson. "Howard." *Truth in Comedy: The Manual of Improvisation*. Colorado Springs, CO: Meriwether, 1994.

Hass, Robert. *The Essential Haiku: Versions of Basho, Buson & Issa*. New York: Ecco, 1994.

Hoey, Michael. *Lexical Priming*. London: Routledge, 2005.

Hymes, Dell H. "Models of the Interaction of Language and Social Life." In: Gumperz and Hymes, 35–71.

James, William. *The Heart of William James*. Edited and with an introduction by Robert Richardson. Cambridge, MA: Harvard University Press, 2010.

Kneece, Jack. *Ghost Army of World War II*. Gretna, LA: Pelican, 2001.

O'Rourke, Kevin. *The Book of Korean Shijo*. Cambridge, MA: Harvard University Asia Center, 2002.

Remer, Theodore G. (ed.). *Serendipity and the Three Princes, from the Peregrinaggio of 1557*. Norman: University of Oklahoma Press, 1965.

Rutt, Richard. *The Bamboo Grove: An Introduction to Sijo*. Ann Arbor: University of Michigan Press, 1998.

Silver, Sean. "The Prehistory of Serendipity, from Bacon to Walpole." *Isis* 106(2), 2015: 235–256.

Ueda, Makoto. *Basho and His Interpreters: Selected Hokku with Commentary*. Stanford: Stanford University Press, 1991.

MY NAME IS WIT

Works Cited

91 **"The clown is the wit of action":** W. H. Auden, "Notes on the Comic." *Thought* 27(1), Spring 1952: 64.

91 **"Because I got odium upon myself before coming here":** Cited in W. B. Stanford, *The Ulysses Theme: A Study in the Adaptability of a Traditional Hero* (Dallas: Spring Publications, 1992), 11.

93 **"a complex but very coherent body of mental attitudes":** Marcel Detienne and Jean-Pierre Vernant, *Cunning Intelligence in Greek Culture and Society* (Chicago: University of Chicago Press, 1991), 3–4.

94 **The Frog People had dammed the river:** Erdoes and Ortiz, 355–356.

94 **Like clowns:** Towsen, 12.

95 **During the many misadventures of Mica:** Kimberly A. Christen (ed.), *Clowns and Tricksters: An Encyclopedia of Tradition and Culture* (Denver: ABC-CLIO, 1998), 145.

96 **Legba had long resented Mawu:** Ibid., 133.

97 **Ten thousand enemy soldiers were fast approaching:** Adapted from Lo Kuan-chung, *Three Kingdoms: China's Epic Drama*, translated from the Chinese and edited by Moss Roberts (New York: Pantheon Books, 1976), 173–178.

99 **Just then Aicha stepped forward:** Adapted from Marilyn Jurich, *Scheherazade's Sisters: Trickster Heroines and Their Stories in World Literature* (Westport, CT: Greenwood Press, 1998), 108; Dan Keding, *Elder Tales: Stories of Wisdom and Courage from Around the World* (Westport, CT: Libraries Unlimited, 2008), 55–56.

100 **Tenali Rama displayed an unusually shrewd:** Adapted from Pandit S. M. Natesa Sastri, *Tales of Tennalirama: The Famous Court Jester of Southern India* (Madras: G. A. Natesan, 1900), 1–3; Ramanujan, 206; Lee Siegel, *Laughing Matters: Comic Tradition in India* (Chicago: University of Chicago Press, 1987), 18–19.

102 **One day, San Pedro found some figs in a bag:** Adapted from Ruth Warner Giddings, *Yaqui Myths and Legends* (Tucson: Anthropological Papers of the University of Arizona, no. 2, 1959), 48, 182.

104 **King Akbar received a handsome, eloquent parrot as a gift:** Adapted from Siegel, 309–310. With apologies to Monty Python's dead parrot sketch.

Works Consulted

Barnouw, Jeffrey. *Odysseus, Hero of Practical Intelligence: Deliberation and Signs in Homer's Odyssey*. Lanham, MD: University Press of America, 2004.

Beyer, Rick, and Elizabeth Sayles. *The Ghost Army of World War II*. New York: Princeton Architectural Press, 2015.

Bright, William. *A Coyote Reader*. Berkeley: University of California Press, 1993.

Brown, Norman O. *Hermes the Thief: The Evolution of A Myth*. New York: Vintage Books, 1969.

Christen, Kimberly A. (ed.). *Clowns and Tricksters: An Encyclopedia of Tradition and Culture*. Denver: ABC-CLIO, 1998.

Courlander, Harold. *A Treasury of African Folklore*. New York: Crown, 1975.

Detienne, Marcel, and Jean-Pierre Vernant. *Cunning Intelligence in Greek Culture and Society*. Chicago: University of Chicago Press, 1991.

El-Shamy, Hasan M. (ed.). *Folktales of Egypt*. Chicago: University of Chicago Press, 1980.

Erdoes, Richard, and Alfonso Ortiz (eds). *American Indian Myths and Legends*. New York: Pantheon Books, 1984.

Giddings, Ruth Warner. *Yaqui Myths and Legends*. Tucson: Anthropological Papers of the University of Arizona, no. 2, 1959.

Hurston, Zora Neale. "High John de Conquer." *The American Mercury*, October 1943, 450–458.

Hyde, Lewis. *Trickster Makes This World: Mischief, Myth and Art*. New York: Farrar, Straus and Giroux, 2010.

Hynes, William J., and William G. Doty (eds.). *Mythical Trickster Figures: Contours, Contexts and Criticisms*. Tuscaloosa and London: University of Alabama Press, 1993.

Landay, Lori. *Madcaps, Screwballs, and Con Women: The Female Trickster in American Culture*. Philadelphia: University of Pennsylvania Press, 1998.

Otto, Beatrice K. *Fools Are Everywhere: The Court Jester Around the World*. Chicago: University of Chicago Press, 2001.

Pelton, Robert D. *The Trickster in West Africa: A Study of Mythic Irony and Sacred Delight*. Berkeley: University of California Press, 1980.

Radin, Paul. *The Trickster: A Study in American Indian Mythology*. London: Routledge and Kegan Paul, 1956.

Ramanujan, A. K. *Folktales from India: A Selection of Oral Tales from Twenty-two Languages*. New York: Pantheon Books, 1991.

Robinson, Edward Jewitt. *Tales and Poems of South India*. London: T. Woolmer, 1885.

Shulman, David Dean. *The King and the Clown in South Indian Myth and Poetry*. Princeton: Princeton University Press, 1985.

Siegel, Lee. *Laughing Matters: Comic Tradition in India*. Chicago: University of Chicago Press, 1987.

Stanford, W. B. *The Ulysses Theme: A Study in the Adaptability of a Traditional Hero*. Dallas: Spring Publications, 1992.

Towsen, John H. *Clowns*. New York: Hawthorn Books, 1976.

Warde, Frederick. *The Fools of Shakespeare: An Interpretation of Their Wit, Wisdom and Personalities*. London: McBride, Nast, 1915.

Welsford, Enid. *The Fool: His Social and Literary History*. Garden City, NY: Anchor Books, 1961.

Williams, David. *The Trickster Brain: Neuroscience, Evolution, and Narrative*. Lanham, MD: Lexington Books, 2012.

SLAPSTICK METAPHYSICS

Works Cited

105 **"A jest is tried as powder is—the most sudden is the best":** P. M. Zall (ed.), *A Nest of Ninnies, and Other English Jestbooks of the Seventeenth Century* (Lincoln: University of Nebraska Press, 1970), 75.

106 **Heard the one about the German:** William Novak and Moshe Waldoks (eds.), *The Big Book of Jewish Humor: 25th Anniversary* (New York: HarperCollins, 2006), XXVIII.

106 **I read this short story once, by Isaac Asimov:** Isaac Asimov, "Jokester," in *The Complete Stories*, vol. 1 (New York: Broadway Books), 123–134.

108 **Every pitcher throws the same ball:** "Let no one say that I have said nothing new: the arrangement of the material is new. When playing tennis, both players hit the same ball, but one of them places it better." Blaise Pascal. Cited in Geary, 279.

109 **Whoever wiped away the ink got the job:** Keith Johnstone, *Impro: Improvisation and the Theatre* (London: Methuen Drama, 1979), 92.

110 **the fox that found a hole in the henhouse fence:** Hyam Maccoby, *The Day God Laughed: Sayings, Fables and Entertainments of the Jewish Sages* (London: Robson Books, 1978), 69.

111 **Pinchie Winchie:** Harpo Marx, with Rowland Barber, *Harpo Speaks* (New York: Limelight Editions, 1985), 277–281.

111 **Harpo is kind of idly playing with a pack of matches:** Ibid., 473–474.

112 **Heard the one about the Muslim guru Mullah Nasruddin?:** Adapted from Enid Welsford, *The Fool: His Social and Literary History* (Garden City, NY: Anchor Books, 1961), 29.

Works Consulted

Blesh, Rudi. *Keaton*. London: Secker & Warburg, 1967.

Blyth, R. H. *Japanese Humour*. Tokyo: Japan Travel Bureau, 1957.

Cazamian, Louis. *The Development of English Humor, Parts I and II*. Durham: Duke University Press, 1952.

Chafe, Wallace. *The Importance of Not Being Earnest: The Feeling Behind Laughter and Humor*. Amsterdam and Philadelphia: John Benjamins, 2007.

Cohen, Ted. *Jokes: Philosophical Thoughts on Joking Matters*. Chicago: University of Chicago Press, 1999.

Dardis, Tom. *Keaton: The Man Who Wouldn't Lie Down*. New York: Charles Scribner's Sons, 1979.

Eastman, Max. *Enjoyment of Laughter*. New York: Simon and Schuster, 1936.

El Eflaki, Shemsu-'D-Din Ahmed. *Legends of the Sufis. From the Work Entitled The Acts of the Adepts*. Translated by James W. Redhouse. London: Theosophical Publishing House, 1976.

Fry, Jr., William F. *Sweet Madness: A Study of Humor*. Palo Alto: Pacific Books, 1963.

Grotjahn, Martin. *Beyond Laughter: Humor and the Subconscious*. New York: McGraw-Hill, 1966.

Hugill, Beryl. *Bring on the Clowns*. London: David & Charles, 1980.

Hurley, Matthew M., Daniel C. Dennett, and Reginald B. Adams, Jr. *Inside Jokes: Using Humor to Reverse-Engineer the Mind*. Cambridge, MA: MIT Press, 2011.

Hyers, Conrad. *The Laughing Buddha: Zen and the Comic Spirit*. Wolfeboro, NH: Longwood Academic, 1989.

Johnstone, Keith. *Impro: Improvisation and the Theatre*. London: Methuen Drama, 1979.

Keaton, Buster, with Charles Samuels. *My Wonderful World of Slapstick*. Garden City, NY: Doubleday, 1960.

Lukc, Sir Harry. *An Eastern Chequerboard*. London: Lovat Dickson, 1934.

Maccoby, Hyam. *The Day God Laughed: Sayings, Fables and Entertainments of the Jewish Sages*. London: Robson Books, 1978.

Monro, D. H. "Theories of Humor." In: *Writing and Reading Across the Curriculum*. Behrens, Laurence, and Leonard J. Rosen (eds.). Glenview, IL: Scott, Foresman, 1988, 349–355.

Morreall, John. *Taking Laughter Seriously*. Albany: State University of New York, 1983.

———. *Comic Relief: A Comprehensive Philosophy of Humor*. Chichester: Wiley-Blackwell, 2009.

Nicolson, Harold. *The English Sense of Humor and Other Essays*. New York: Funk & Wagnalls, 1968.

Oring, Elliott. *Jokes and Their Relations*. Lexington: University Press of Kentucky, 1992.

Pirandello, Luigi. *On Humor*. Chapel Hill: University of North Carolina Press, 1960.

Shah, Idries. *Tales of the Dervishes: Teaching-Stories of the Sufi Masters over the Past Thousand Years*. New York: E. P. Dutton, 1970.

Spencer, Herbert. "The Physiology of Laughter." *Macmillan's Magazine* 1, 1860: 395–402.

THE CHAINS OF HABIT

Works Cited

113 **"An ambiguity, in ordinary speech":** William Empson, *Seven Types of Ambiguity* (New York: New Directions, 1966), 1.

113 **On the campus of Cornell University:** Daniel J. Simons and Daniel T. Levin, "Failure to Detect Changes to People during a Real-World Interaction." *Psychonomic Bulletin & Review* 5(4), 1998: 644–649.

115 **"It is the expected that happens":** Joseph Jastrow, "The Mind's Eye." *Popular Science Monthly* 54, 1899: 303.

116 **"We see the object as though it were enveloped":** Victor Shklovsky, "Art as Technique," in *Russian Formalist Criticism: Four Essays*, translated and with an introduction by Lee T. Melon and Marion J. Reis (Lincoln: University of Nebraska Press, 1965), 12.

116 **"Art removes objects from the automatism of perception":** Ibid., 13.

116 **"Art exists that one may recover the sensation of life":** Ibid., 12.

118 **a worker wielding a hammer:** Jan Plamper, "Abolishing Ambiguity: Soviet Censorship Practices in the 1930s," *The Russian Review* 60, October 2001: 537.

118 **Sergei Kirov's ambiguous finger:** Ibid., 535.

119 **the front page of *Southern Metropolis News*:** Nectar Gan, "Editor at Liberal Chinese Newspaper Fired for Xi Front Page." *South China Morning Post*, March 2, 2016.

120 **"fruit language" and the crackdown:** Perry Link, *An Anatomy of*

Chinese: Rhythm, Metaphor, Politics (Cambridge, MA: Harvard University Press, 2013), 246.

121 **"Janusian thinking":** Albert Rothenberg, "Janusian Process,"in M. A. Runco and S. R. Pritzker (eds.), *Encyclopedia of Creativity*, vol. 2 (San Diego: Academic Press, 1999), 103–108.

121 **"no question of a choice between two different concepts":** Ibid., 105.

122 **multiple-object tracking (MOT) experiments:** Brian J. Scholl, "What Have We Learned about Attention from Multiple-Object Tracking (and Vice Versa)?" in D. Dedrick and L. Trick (eds.), *Computation, Cognition, and Pylyshyn* (Cambridge, MA: MIT Press, 2009), 49–78.

122 **researchers showed participants photographs:** Claudia Muth, Vera M. Hesslinger, and Claus-Christian Carbon, "The Appeal of Challenge in the Perception of Art: How Ambiguity, Solvability of Ambiguity, and the Opportunity for Insight Affect Appreciation." *Psychology of Aesthetics, Creativity, and the Arts* 9(3), 2015: 206–216.

123 **This study followed earlier research by the same team:** Claudia Muth and Claus-Christian Carbon. "The Aesthetic Aha: On the Pleasure of Having Insights into Gestalt." *Acta Psychol* 144(1), 2013: 25–30.

Works Consulted

Blasko, Vincent J., and Michael P. Mokwa. "Creativity in Advertising: A Janusian Perspective." *Journal of Advertising* 15(4), 1986: 43–72.

Blumenthal, Arthur L. "The Intrepid Joseph Jastrow." In: Kimble, Gregory A., Michael Wertheimer, and Charlotte White (eds.). *Portraits of Pioneers in Psychology*. Hillsdale, NJ: Lawrence Erlbaum, 1991.

Empson, William. *The Structure of Complex Words*. Cambridge, MA: Harvard University Press, 1989.

———. *Seven Types of Ambiguity*. New York: New Directions, 1966.

James, William. *The Heart of William James*. Edited and with an introduction by Robert Richardson. Cambridge, MA: Harvard University Press, 2010.

Jastrow, Joseph. "The Mind's Eye." *Popular Science Monthly* 54, 1899: 299–312.

Lemon, Lee T., and Marion J. Reis (eds.). *Russian Formalist Criticism: Four Essays*. Lincoln and London: University of Nebraska Press, 1965.

Palmer, S. E. *Vision Science: Photons to Phenomenology*. Cambridge, MA: MIT Press, 1999.

Rothenberg, Albert. "Janusian Process" (1999). In: *Encyclopedia of Creativ-*

ity, Volume 2. Runco, M. A., and S. R. Pritzker (eds.). San Diego: Academic Press, 2011, 103–108.

———. "The Process of Janusian Thinking in Creativity." *Archives of General Psychiatry* 24(3), 1971: 195–205.

Shapiro, Kimron L., et al. "The Attentional Blink." *Trends in Cognitive Neurosciences* 1(8), 1997: 291–296.

FINDING MINDS

Works Cited

125 **"What a lucky find reveals first":** Lewis Hyde, *Trickster Makes This World: Mischief, Myth and Art* (New York: Farrar, Straus and Giroux, 2010), 139.

125 **the structure of the pun . . . is identical to that of other:** L. G. Heller, "Toward a General Typology of the Pun," in Marvin K. L. Ching, Michael C. Haley, and Ronald F. Lunsford (eds.), *Linguistic Perspectives on Literature* (London and Boston: Routledge & Kegan Paul, 1980), 306.

126 **Alfredo Moser, . . . looking for an alternative to matches:** Navi Radjou, Jaideep Prabhu, and Simone Ahuja. *Jugaad Innovation: Think Frugal, Be Flexible, Generate Breakthrough Growth* (San Francisco: Jossey-Bass, 2012), 112–113.

126 **The story of the word "serendipity":** Leo A. Goodman, "Notes on the Etymology of Serendipity and Some Related Philological Observations." *Modern Language Notes* 76(5), May 1961: 454–457.

126 **the tale of the Three Princes of Serendip:** Adapted from Theodore G. Remer (ed.), *Serendipity and the Three Princes, from the Peregrinaggio of 1557* (Norman: University of Oklahoma Press, 1965), 57–65.

128 **by accident and sagacity:** Horace Walpole, *The Yale Edition of Horace Walpole's Correspondence*, vol. 26, W. S. Lewis, ed. (New Haven: Yale University Press, 1937–1983), 34.

128 **Poe's "The Murders in the Rue Morgue":** Edgar Allan Poe, "The Murders in the Rue Morgue," in *The Collected Tales and Poems of Edgar Allan Poe* (London: Wordsworth Editions, 2009), 2–26.

129 **"the difference in the extent of the information obtained":** Ibid., 3.

129 **insulin as the hormone that metabolizes glucose from carbohydrates:** Royston M. Roberts, *Serendipity: Accidental Discoveries in Science* (New York: John Wiley & Sons, 1989), 123; and Remer, 170.

130 **"In the fields of observation":** Roberts, 244.

130 **"gorgeous nuptial colors":** Nikolaas Tinbergen, *The Herring Gull's World: A Study of the Social Behaviour of Birds* (New York: Harper & Row, 1971), 219–220.

131 **first-class noticers:** Max Bazerman, "Becoming a First-Class Noticer: How to Spot and Prevent Ethical Failures in Your Organization," *Harvard Business Review* 92(7/8), July–August 2014: 116–119.

131 ***bricoleurs:*** Claude Lévi-Strauss, *The Savage Mind* (London: Weidenfeld and Nicolson, 1962), 16–18.

131 **When you live abroad, everything is different:** William W. Maddux and Adam D. Galinsky, "Cultural Borders and Mental Barriers: The Relationship Between Living Abroad and Creativity." *Journal of Personality and Social Psychology* 96(5), 2009: 1047–1061.

132 **the Unusual Uses Test:** J. P. Guilford, *The Nature of Human Intelligence* (New York: McGraw-Hill, 1967).

133 **the *hagelslag* experiment and "schema violations":** Simone M. Ritter et al., "Diversifying Experiences Enhance Cognitive Flexibility." *Journal of Experimental Social Psychology* 48(4), July 2012: 961–964.

134 **"make a dummy that would stimulate the chick":** Tinbergen, *The Herring Gull's World*, 206.

134 **"supernormal stimuli . . . offer stimulus situations":** Nikolaas Tinbergen, *The Study of Instinct* (Oxford: Oxford University Press, 1958), 44.

135 **"Deeply rooted in man":** Tinbergen, *The Herring Gull's World*, 222.

135 **"Humor at its best":** Cited in Max Eastman, *The Enjoyment of Laughter* (New York: Simon and Schuster, 1936), 270.

Works Consulted

Bacon, Francis. *Wisdom of the Ancients.* In: *The Moral and Historical Works of Lord Bacon.* London: Henry G. Bohn, 1860.

Barrett, Deirdre. *Supernormal Stimuli: How Primal Urges Overran Their Evolutionary Purpose.* New York: W. W. Norton, 2010.

Garrett, Alfred B. *The Flash of Genius.* Princeton, NJ: D. Van Nostrand, 1963.

Heller, L. G. "Toward a General Typology of the Pun." In: *Linguistic Perspectives on Literature.* Ching, Marvin K. L., Michael C. Haley, and Ronald F. Lunsford (eds.). London and Boston: Routledge & Kegan Paul, 1980, 305–318.

Heller, L. G., and James Macris. *Multilateral Allovariance.* London: Theoretical Publications of the International Linguistic Association, no. 1, 1972.

Lévi-Strauss, Claude. *The Savage Mind.* London: Weidenfeld and Nicolson, 1962.

Merton, Robert K., and Elinor Barber. *The Travels and Adventures of Serendipity: A Study in Sociological Semantics and the Sociology of Science.* Princeton, NJ: Princeton University Press, 2004.

Radjou, Navi, Jaideep Prabhu, and Simone Ahuja. *Jugaad Innovation: Think Frugal, Be Flexible, Generate Breakthrough Growth.* San Francisco: Jossey-Bass, 2012.

Remer, Theodore G. (ed.). *Serendipity and the Three Princes, from the Peregrinaggio of 1557.* Norman: University of Oklahoma Press, 1965.

Roberts, Royston M. *Serendipity: Accidental Discoveries in Science.* New York: John Wiley & Sons, 1989.

Silver, Sean. "The Prehistory of Serendipity, from Bacon to Walpole." *Isis* 106(2), 2015: 235–256.

Sneader, Walter. *Drug Discovery: A History.* New York: John Wiley, 2005.

Tinbergen, Nikolaas. *The Herring Gull's World: A Study of the Social Behaviour of Birds.* New York: Harper & Row, 1971.

———. *The Study of Instinct.* Oxford: Oxford University Press, 1958.

AMBIGUOUS FIGURES

Works Cited

136 **"Discovery consists of seeing":** Cited in Royston M. Roberts, *Serendipity: Accidental Discoveries in Science* (New York: John Wiley & Sons, 1989), 245.

137 **"True seeing, observing, is a double process":** Jastrow, 300.

138 **human faces in rock outcroppings:** The Chinsekikan (Hall of Curious Rocks) Museum, in Chichibu, Japan, contains some 1,700 rocks that resemble human faces.

138 **"opening the mind"** . . . **"If you look":** Cited in Joshua Charles Taylor (ed.). *Nineteenth-Century Theories of Art* (Berkeley: University of California Press, 1987), 65.

139 **"the human eye detects and often creates the resemblances":** Jastrow, 300.

141 **"Seeing is not wholly an objective matter":** Ibid., 311.

141 **children shown the duck-rabbit around Easter:** P. Brugger and S. Brugger, "The Easter Bunny in October: Is It Disguised as a Duck?" *Perceptual and Motor Skills* 76, 1993: 577–578.

144 **"Have you ever been alive?":** Cited in Silvano Levy, "Obituary: Marcel Marien." *The Independent.* October 1, 1993.

146 **he fooled visitors to his home on the outskirts of Tokyo:** Steven Heller, "Shigeo Fukuda, Graphic Designer, Dies at 76." *New York Times,* January 19, 2009, A31.

Works Consulted

Bürgi, Bernhard, and Toni Stooss. *Markus Raetz: Arbeiten 1962 bis 1986.* Zürich: Kunsthaus Zürich, 1986.

Canonne, Xavier. *Surrealism in Belgium: The Discreet Charm of the Bourgeoisie.* Brussels: Marot S. A. and Berklet Editions, 2015.

Fukuda, Shigeo. *Masterworks.* Buffalo, NY: Firefly Books, 2005.

———. *Visual Illusion.* Tokyo: Rikuyosha, 1982.

Heller, Stephen, and Gail Anderson. *Graphic Wit: The Art of Humor in Design.* New York: Watson-Guptill, 1991.

Hughes, Patrick. *More on Oxymoron: Foolish Wisdom in Words and Pictures.* London: Penguin Books, 1983.

———. *Paradoxymoron.* London: Reverspective, 2011.

Hughes, Patrick, and George Brecht. *Vicious Circles and Infinity: An Anthology of Paradoxes.* London: Penguin Books, 1975.

Kince, Eli. *Visual Puns in Design: The Pun Used as a Communication Tool.* New York: Watson-Guptill, 1982.

McAlhone, Beryl, and David Stuart. *A Smile in the Mind: Witty Thinking in Graphic Design.* London: Phaidon, 2001.

Penrose, L., and R. Penrose. "Impossible Objects: A Special Type of Visual Illusion." *British Journal of Psychology* 49(1), 1958: 31–33.

Sarcone, Gianni A., and Marie-Jo Waeber. *Fantastic Optical Illusions: Over 150 Original Deceptive Images, Visual Tricks and Optical Puzzles.* London: Carlton Books, 2006.

Seckel, Al. *Masters of Deception: Escher, Dalí, and the Artists of Optical Illusion.* New York: Fall River, 2010.

Tucker, Marcia. *Markus Raetz: In the Realm of the Possible.* New York: New Museum of Contemporary Art, 1988.

WISDOM OF THE SAGES

Works Cited

150 **"As iron sharpeneth iron, so minds sharpen minds":** Proverbs 27:17.

150 **One day a friend invited Hershele Ostropoler:** Adapted from Rufus Learsi, *Filled with Laughter: A Fiesta of Jewish Folk Humor* (New York: Thomas Yoseloff, 1961), 166–167.

152 **Kyogen Osho's story of a man up a tree:** Katsuki Sekida (trans.), *Two Zen Classics: Mumonkan & Hekiganroku* (New York: Weatherhill, 1977), 38.

153 **Once, at dinner, when Rabbi Barukh was too depressed:** David

A. Chapin and Ben Weinstock, *The Road from Letichev: The History and Culture of a Forgotten Jewish Community in Eastern Europe*, vol.1 (Lincoln, NE: Writer's Showcase, 2000), 81.

154 **So it is said of Brother Groucho:** Joseph Telushkin, *Jewish Humor: What the Best Jewish Jokes Say about the Jews* (New York: William Morrow, 1992), 109.

154 **"reciprocal interference":** Henri Bergson, "Laughter: An Essay on the Meaning of the Comic," in *Comedy*, Wylie Sypher (ed.) (New York: Doubleday Anchor Books, 1956), 123.

154 **John Scogan, having greatly offended Edward IV:** Christen, 94.

154 **"One of the most fruitful devices of wit":** Auden, 64–65.

155 **"What separates you from a pig is what I'd like to know":** Chapin and Weinstock, 79–84.

155 **Having hired Harpo and Chico:** From the 1933 Marx Brothers film *Duck Soup*.

156 **When Pastor Gregory was denied service:** From Dick Gregory's 1961 album *In Living Black & White*.

156 **"Such sallies are believed to be movements of the character":** Aristotle, *Nicomachean Ethics*, translated and with an introduction and notes by Martin Ostwald (Indianapolis: Bobbs-Merrill Educational, 1979), 107.

156 **Mathurine accompanying a lady of the court:** Towsen, 24–25.

156 **Wile E. Coyote (*Carnivorus vulgaris*):** From the 1952 Merrie Melodies cartoon *Going! Going! Gosh!*

157 **the benign violation theory:** A. P. McGraw and C. Warren, "Benign Violation Theory." *Encyclopedia of Humor Studies* (Thousand Oaks, CA: Sage, 2014), 75–77.

157 **"Too fucking busy, and vice versa":** Cited in Oscar Levant, *The Unimportance of Being Oscar* (New York: G. P. Putnam's Sons, 1968), 89.

157 **So it is written in the Book of Isaac:** Adapted from the Isaac Asimov short story "Jokester" in Isaac Asimov, *The Complete Stories*, vol. 1 (New York: Broadway Books, 1990), 123.

158 **"What does it say to you?":** From Woody Allen's 1972 film *Play It Again, Sam*.

159 **When Chelmites were injuring themselves:** Steve Sanfield, *The Feather Merchants and Other Tales of the Fools of Chelm* (New York: Orchard Books, 1991), 85.

159 **When storms continually damaged the town's new sundial:** Ibid., 52.

159 **There once was a man who lived in deathly fear:** Burton Watson (trans.), *The Complete Works of Chuang Tzu* (New York: Columbia University Press, 1968), 348.

160 **One day, in a small town in the county of Jianzhou:** Stefan H. Verstappen, *The Thirty-Six Strategies of Ancient China* (San Francisco: China Books & Periodicals, 1999), 60.

160 **Clamor in the east; attack in the west:** Ibid., 27.

160 **Lure your opponent onto the roof:** Ibid., 141.

160 **It is as if a beneficent king:** Goldin, 116.

161 **And so it is told of Tokusan:** Sekida, 93.

161 **In the old city of Jerusalem lived a baker:** From Shoofly: An Audiomagazine for Children, vol. 1, no. 1, October, 1994.

162 **Practical wisdom:** See Aristotle, *Nicomachean Ethics*, 154.

162 **a shovelful of fleas:** Adapted from a saying by Abraham Lincoln, in Zall, 28.

162 **"I beg you, master, pacify my mind":** Sekida, 118.

162 **To a carrot:** Otto, 164.

162 **Therefore, if thou seest a person of wit:** Goldin, 9.

162 **a priest, an imam, and a rabbi:** Egon Larsen, *Wit as a Weapon: The Political Joke in History* (London: Frederick Muller, 1980), 78.

Works Consulted

Aristotle. *Nicomachean Ethics*. Translated, with an introduction and notes, by Martin Ostwald. Indianapolis: Bobbs-Merrill Educational, 1979.

Asimov, Isaac. *Isaac Asimov's Treasury of Humor: A Lifetime Collection of Favorite Jokes, Anecdotes, and Limericks with Copious Notes on How to Tell Them and Why*. Boston: Houghton Mifflin, 1971.

Bermant, Chaim. *What's the Joke? A Study of Jewish Humor through the Ages*. London: Weidenfeld and Nicolson, 1986.

Cleary, Thomas (trans. and ed.). *Mastering the Art of War: Zhuge Liang's and Liu Ji's Commentaries on the Classic by Sun Tzu*. Boston: Shambhala, 1989.

Elson, John James (ed.). *The Wits, or, Sport upon Sport*. Ithaca: Cornell University Press, 1932.

Fix, Charlene. *Harpo Marx as Trickster*. Jefferson, NC: McFarland, 2013.

Friedman, Hershey H., and Linda Weiser Friedman. *God Laughed: Sources of Jewish Humor*. New Brunswick, NJ: Transaction, 2014.

Goldin, Judah. *The Living Talmud: The Wisdom of the Fathers and Its Classical Commentaries, Selected and Translated with an Essay by Judah Goldin*. New York: New American Library, 1957.

Harris, Leon A. *The Fine Art of Political Wit*. New York: E. P. Dutton, 1964.

Hugill, Beryl. *Bring on the Clowns*. London: David & Charles, 1980.

Jones, Chuck. *Chuck Amuck: The Life and Times of an Animated Cartoonist*. New York: Farrar, Straus and Giroux, 1989.

Kenner, Hugh. *Chuck Jones: A Flurry of Drawings.* Berkeley: University of California Press, 1994.

———. *The Counterfeiters: An Historical Comedy.* Baltimore: Johns Hopkins University Press, 1985.

Larsen, Egon. *Wit as a Weapon: The Political Joke in History.* London: Frederick Muller, 1980.

Learsi, Rufus. *Filled with Laughter: A Fiesta of Jewish Folk Humor.* New York: Thomas Yoseloff, 1961.

Levy, Solomon. *Treasures of the Talmud.* Maple Shade, NJ: Genizah Editions, 2001.

Maccoby, Hyam. *The Day God Laughed: Sayings, Fables and Entertainments of the Jewish Sages.* London: Robson Books, 1978.

Nisker, Wes "Scoop." *The Essential Crazy Wisdom.* Berkeley: Ten Speed Press, 2001.

Novak, William, and Moshe Waldoks (eds.). *The Big Book of Jewish Humor: 25th Anniversary.* New York: HarperCollins, 2006.

Olsvanger, Immanuel. *Royte Pomerantsen.* New York: Schocken Books, 1965.

Reik, Theodor. *Jewish Wit.* New York: Gamut Press, 1962.

Sekida, Katsuki (trans.) *Two Zen Classics: Mumonkan & Hekiganroku.* New York: Weatherhill, 1977.

Telushkin, Joseph. *Jewish Humor: What the Best Jewish Jokes Say about the Jews.* New York: William Morrow, 1992.

Tenenbaum, Samuel. *The Wise Men of Chelm.* New York: Thomas Yoseloff, 1965.

Verstappen, Stefan H. *The Thirty-Six Strategies of Ancient China.* San Francisco: China Books & Periodicals, 1999.

Wardroper, John. *Jest upon Jest: A Selection from the Jestbooks and Collections of Merry Tales Published from the Reign of Richard III to George III.* London: Routledge & Kegan Paul, 1970.

Watson, Burton (trans.). *The Complete Works of Chuang Tzu.* New York: Columbia University Press, 1968.

TRUE WIT

Works Cited

163 **"The rose is obsolete":** William Carlos Williams, "Spring and All," in *Imaginations* (New York: New Directions, 1971), 107.

163 **PROCLAMATION:** This chapter is based on the "Proclamation" published in the literary magazine *Transition*, no. 16–17, June 1929, 13.

164 **"Just as watch-makers usually provide"**: Freud, *Jokes and Their Relationship to the Unconscious*, 135.

164 **"Wit is a State of Imagination"**: Cited in D. Judson Milburn, *The Age of Wit, 1650–1750* (New York: Macmillan, 1966), 289–290.

164 **"The sign of a first-rate intelligence"**: F. Scott Fitzgerald, "The Crack-Up." *Esquire*, February 1936, 41.

164 **"This fellow's wise enough to play the fool"**: Shakespeare, William. *Twelfth Night*, iii.I.67.

164 **"We consider wit as a sort of feat or trick"**: Cited in Stuart M. Tave, *The Amiable Humorist: A Study in the Comic Theory and Criticism of the Eighteenth and Early Nineteenth Centuries* (Chicago: University of Chicago Press, 1960), 66.

165 **"What beauty is for the eyes"**: Cited in K. K. Ruthven, *The Conceit* (London: Methuen, 1969), 139.

165 **"How lovely are the wiles of Words!"**: Cited in Michael West, *Transcendental Wordplay: America's Romantic Punsters and the Search for the Language of Nature* (Athens: Ohio University Press, 2000), 334.

Works Consulted

De Cesare, Mario A. (ed.). *George Herbert and the Seventeenth-Century Religious Poets*. New York: W. W. Norton, 1978.

Milburn, D. Judson. *The Age of Wit, 1650–1750*. New York: Macmillan, 1966.

Ruthven, K. K. *The Conceit*. London: Methuen, 1969.

Tave, Stuart M. *The Amiable Humorist: A Study in the Comic Theory and Criticism of the Eighteenth and Early Nineteenth Centuries*. Chicago: University of Chicago Press, 1960.

WIT'S END

Works Cited

166 **"All things are big with jest"**: George Herbert, *The Complete English Poems*. Edited by John Tobin (London: Penguin Press, 1991), 14.

167 **Abba Theophilus, the archbishop, came to Scetis**: Benedicta Ward (trans.), *The Sayings of the Desert Fathers: The Alphabetical Collection* (Kalamazoo, MI: Cistercian, 1975), 81.

169 **"lines of ponderation"**: Cited in Hugh H. Grady, "Rhetoric, Wit, and Art in Gracián's Agudeza." *Modern Language Quarterly* 41(1), 1980: 24.

169 **the kind of sermon that stranger heard who, passing**: Watkins, 81–82.

170 **"because people by what they understand are best led":** Herbert, 204.

170 **the kind of sermon that informs:** Ibid., 232.

170 **Like the story of the disciple of a famous Sufi master:** Adapted from Idries Shah, *Tales of the Dervishes: Teaching-Stories of the Sufi Masters over the Past Thousand Years* (New York: E. P. Dutton, 1970), 191.

171 **"What is attended with difficulty":** Augustine, *On Christian Doctrine*, cited in Ryan Topping, *Renewing the Mind: A Reader in the Philosophy of Catholic Education* (Washington, DC: Catholic University of America Press, 2015), 45.

171 **we are more original and open-minded:** Matthijs Baas et al., "A Meta-Analysis of 25 Years of Mood-Creativity Research: Hedonic Tone, Activation, or Regulatory Focus." *Psychological Bulletin* 134(6), 2008: 779–806.

172 **"laughter is the beginning of prayer":** Cited in M. Conrad Hyers (ed.), *Holy Laughter: Essays in The Comic Perspective* (New York: Seabury Press, 1969), 134.

172 **Wit, like faith, beholds with equanimity:** Reinhold Niebuhr, "Humor and Faith," Hyers, 135.

172 **why angels can fly:** "Angels can fly because they take themselves lightly," G. K. Chesterton.

173 **"soft, tenuous liquid":** Ludovico Ariosto, *Orlando Furioso* (Oxford: Oxford University Press, 2008), 420.

173 **the story of that wealthy merchant:** Cleophus J. LaRue, *Power in the Pulpit: How America's Most Effective Black Preachers Prepare Their Sermons* (Louisville: Westminster John Know Press, 2002), 55–56.

174 **"The most difficult thing to find is the way to the signposts":** Geary, 20.

Works Consulted

Bell, Aubrey F. G. *Baltasar Gracián*. Oxford: Oxford University Press, 1921.

Buttrick, David. *Homiletic Moves and Structures*. Minneapolis: Fortress Press, 1987.

De Cesare, Mario A. (ed.). *George Herbert and the Seventeenth-Century Religious Poets*. New York: W. W. Norton, 1978.

Foster, Virginia Ramos. *Baltasar Gracián*. Boston: Twayne, 1975.

Grady, Hugh H. "Rhetoric, Wit, and Art in Gracián's Agudeza." *Modern Language Quarterly* 41(1), 1980: 21–37.

Hatcher, William E. *John Jasper: The Unmatched Negro Philosopher and Preacher.* New York: Negro Universities Press, 1969.

Herbert, George. *The Complete English Poems.* Edited by John Tobin. London: Penguin Press, 1991.

Hyers, M. Conrad (ed.). *Holy Laughter: Essays in the Comic Perspective.* New York: Seabury Press, 1969.

LaRue, Cleophus J. *Power in the Pulpit: How America's Most Effective Black Preachers Prepare Their Sermons.* Louisville: Westminster John Know Press, 2002.

Massey, James Earl. *Designing the Sermon: Order and Movement in Preaching.* Nashville: Abingdon Press, 1980.

May, Rollo. *The Courage to Create.* New York: W. W. Norton, 1994.

May, T. E. *Wit of the Golden Age: Articles on Spanish Literature.* Kassel: Edition Reichenberg, 1986.

Mazzeo, Joseph Anthony. *Renaissance and Seventeenth-Century Studies.* New York: Columbia University Press, 1964.

Mitchell, Henry H. *Black Preaching.* Nashville: Abingdon Press, 1970.

Taylor, Gardner C. *How Shall They Preach.* Elgin, IL: Progressive Baptist, 1977.

Woods, M. J. *Gracián Meets Gongora: The Theory and Practice of Wit.* Warminster, UK: Aris & Phillips, 1995.

Zarate Ruiz, Arturo. *Gracián, Wit, and The Baroque Age.* New York: Peter Lang, 1996.

ILLUSTRATION CREDITS

INDEX

Note: Page numbers in *italics* refer to illustrations.